D0065893

WALT KALLESTAD

ENTERTAINMENT EVANGELISM

Taking the Church Public

Abingdon Press

Nashville

ENTERTAINMENT EVANGELISM: TAKING THE CHURCH PUBLIC

Copyright © 1996 by Abingdon Press

This book is printed on recycled, acid-free paper.

Library of Congress Cataloging-in-Publication Data

Kallestad, Walther P., 1948–
    Entertainment evangelism: taking the church public / Walt Kallestad
        p. cm.
    Includes bibliographical references (p.   ).
    ISBN 0-687-05450-8 (hardcover: alk. paper)
    1. Evangelistic work—United States.   2. Popular culture—United States.   3. Popular culture—Religious aspects—Christianity.
    4. United States—Religion—1960—   I. Title.
    BV3773.K35   1996
    261.5—dc20   96-22615
                                                                                      CIP

Scripture quotations, unless otherwise noted, are from the New Revised Standard Version Bible, copyright © 1989, by the Division of Christian Education of the National Council of the Churches of Christ in the United States of America.

Scripture quotations noted KJV are from the King James Version of the Bible.

96 97 98 99 00 01 02 03 04 05—10 9 8 7 6 5 4 3 2 1

MANUFACTURED IN THE UNITED STATES OF AMERICA

To my son,
Patrick Gregory Kallestad,
who has encouraged me to write this book
since his freshman year in college. Thanks for your
encouragement,
your dedication to the ministry of Joy,
and your love for "Pops."

To
Merv Thompson,
my friend and partner in shaping this book.

My wife, Mary, our daughter, Shawn, our staff,
our congregation,
and friends too numerous to list
have supported me tremendously.
Thank you all so very much!

I have become all things to all people,
that I might by all means save some.

—1 Corinthians 9:22*b*

CONTENTS

INTRODUCTION

BANISHING BOREDOM

We have always tried to be guided by the basic idea that, in the discovery of knowledge there is great entertainment—as, conversely, in all good entertainment there is always some grain of wisdom . . . to be gained.

—Walt Disney

My insight emerged rather spontaneously as I drove by a theater when the movie *Batman* was all the rage. Huge crowds were lined up around the block. A few days later I observed similar long lines while waiting to purchase tickets for a concert by one of America's most beloved entertainers, Amy Grant. Then I began noticing images on television of the kind of passion and response given to various rock groups that appear in our community.

These images in the culture forced me to wrestle with the question, If we in the church have the most important, the most exciting, the most revolutionary news in all history, then why don't we find the most creative, innovative, and irresistible ways to capture people's attention so that they will line up to hear, see, and experience it? If we have the gospel of Jesus Christ, the good news, the glad tidings that should go to all the earth, then why is boredom the primary reason people give for not going to church?

Why can't we have even a fraction of the excitement, the passion, the energy, the joy that seem to exude from so many other events in our society? Why can't we do more than merely stifle some yawns in our Christian community as we are attempting to carry out the proclamation of the gospel? If we are called to be a community of joy, why are we so quiet?

An article by Carl Bernstein in *Time* magazine frames the issue for church leaders. Bernstein points out that the world is being saturated with American entertainment products: movies, TV, records, books, sports, and theme parks. By the end of the decade, 50 percent of the money earned by the United States entertainment industry will come from other countries.

Yet this is not just a matter of economic dominance, because America is increasingly being seen as the driving cultural force throughout the world. This is a position it is likely to retain for another one hundred years.

The technical excellence and penchant for the spectacular that characterize American entertainment have universal appeal. Some have argued that American movies, television, and music were the major catalysts in the demise of the totalitarian regimes of Eastern Europe and the USSR.

Perhaps the most important effect of the United States' production, consumption, and exportation of entertainment products is that the distinctions between entertainment, information, communications, and education are becoming less clear. Right now the average American spends forty hours and thirty dollars a week on entertainment. Entertainment is the most used medium in the world (Bernstein, 56-59).

If entertainment is such a force in our world, why don't we utilize this human and cultural vehicle and redeem it for the proclamation of the gospel? Why should we allow our churches to become empty and sterile? Empty cathedrals and sterile church life do little to glorify God.

When I see the kind of entertainment that America is exporting all over the world, I find much of it disturbing. I can envision something different. Why could we not become the center for exporting positive images and values around the world? Do we need to allow destructive entertainment to dominate the culture? Why should not the church develop a style of engaging worship, music, and entertainment that can compete with anything on the market in terms of quality, yet springs from far different values and theological commitments?

The Church as a Filter of Culture

Some church leaders are insulated, and some willfully so, from the forces of competition that define our culture. But I think that we are engaged in a battle for the souls and minds of people and that we must reach out to these persons rather than expecting them to come to us. George Barna puts it this way: "If we hope to include people in the life of the church, we must provide appealing and high quality activities that can successfully compete for people's time, attention and resources. *Church programs should include more entertainment related activities*" (Barna 1990, 93, emphasis added).

Christian churches have a "values filter," through which all activities pass. Thus many adults, especially those with children, depend on the congregation to provide morally acceptable entertainment. That kind of entertainment is increasingly difficult to find.

Entertainment increasingly emerges into new and even strange forms. For instance, image and sound converge into the same experience at a museum in southern California. An exhibit about a five-thousand-year-old culture had an earthquake simulator that allowed people to experience a 5.5 magnitude quake while listening to Carole King's song "I Feel the Earth Move Under My Feet." The museum director says, "This is entertainment. We have to think about presenting this [knowledge] to people in a way that they enjoy it." While it may seem frightening to think of earthquakes as entertaining experiences in southern California, the technique—an appeal to our senses as we are experiencing something awesome—is effective.

The same principle of appeal to sensory experience is found throughout the major reformations of Christian words and deeds. Martin Luther, for example, was no stranger to entertainment. He took tunes that were sung in bars and wrote God-inspired words to go along with the melodies.

While finishing this book, I am lecturing to about one thousand pastors and leaders in Germany. One pastor shares that while living in the geographical heart of Luther's world, it is important that no one forgets the three foundational priniciples Martin Luther believed were essential to making the gospel relevant and applicable to every person. Number one is *simplicity*. Number two is *heartfelt relevancy*. And number three is *entertainment*. These principles are not the gospel; they are simply helpful ways to make the connection.

In Martin Luther's *Table Talk*, he writes, "We ought to direct ourselves in preaching according to the condition of the hearers. . . . To preach plain and simply is a great art: Christ himself talks of tilling ground, of mustard seed. . . . He used altogether homely and simple similitudes" (Luther, 244).

The same practice of borrowing idioms from the culture has been noted in the hymnic language of Charles Wesley. Charles Wesley's hymns eventually became a part of the worship life of more than fifty thousand congregations. They were so popular that successive generations canonized them. Thus much of church music today is only echoing what was effective and highly relevant centuries ago.

The principle is also a biblical one. Many psalms in the Old Testament are based on images and sounds that appear also in the Canaanite culture. The best example is Psalm 29, which many scholars think was a hymn to the Canaanite storm god, Baal. But Israel's hymnist was inspired and decided that this song should be sung to the Lord of all lords. It might have started something like this when the psalmist first laid eyes on it:

> Ascribe to *Baal*, O heavenly beings,
>   ascribe to *Baal* glory and strength.
> Ascribe to *Baal* the glory of his name;
>   worship *Baal* in holy splendor.
> The voice of *Baal* is over the waters;
>   the God of glory thunders,
>   *Baal*, over mighty waters.

Now try reading it by saying *the Lord* instead of *Baal*, and you will be offering praise to our God, who is mightier than any storm.

One Idea on Trial

With many of these thoughts swirling and flowing in and out of my mind and heart, I jotted down some preliminary ideas of how entertainment might enhance the evangelistic mission of our congregation. I did not have time to develop a comprehensive rationale for such comments—I was simply throwing out some ideas for discussion. I wanted to create a dialogue about the issue.

I sent this document to *The Lutheran* magazine, not really imagining that they would actually print it as it was. Mary, my wife, tried to dissuade me from submitting it. Merv Thompson, my friend, thought I was masochistic. Because I have learned over the years not to let fear (or safety) dominate what I do, I submitted it.

When the article became the leading feature of that issue, my life changed dramatically. Reactions to the concept of entertainment evangelism were instantaneous. Many people devoted a great deal of energy and attention to denouncing my "idea," and I soon wished that as much passion could be generated for the unchurched or for our ministry of making Christians.

It was clear that if some of the elite had had access to the twentieth-century equivalent of the stake, I would have been burned at it without hesitation. An article in an Arizona newspaper, *The Verde Independent,* picked up the news:

ENTERTAINMENT ISSUES CAUSE SPLIT AMONG LUTHERANS

"What most churches do on Sunday morning is not working," wrote Rev. Walt Kallestad. "On the other hand, entertainment oriented churches are growing."

Kallestad, whose Lutheran church is known as Community Church of Joy, reaches a Sunday morning congregation of nearly 3,000 by using this entertainment approach. "We may have a stage band, a comedian, clowns, drama, mini-concerts, and other entertainment forms," he said in his column.

What makes a church? "One thing that is always present," said Kallestad, "is a simple, enthusiastic message about the unconditional love, the unlimited grace, and the transforming, cross-centered saving power of Jesus Christ."

If Kallestad thought that would save him from the wrath of his enemies, he was wrong. Letter writers to *The Lutheran* descended on him. "Your church sounds like a teen center on Saturday night." "Give me Christ crucified, not P. T. Barnum." "We don't need a floor show for the bored."

After these letters were published, Kallestad's defenders took up their own cudgels. One writer called Lutheran congregations "The First Church of Frigidaire, in some need of thawing." Another, having read a criticism of Kallestad by a pastor said, "To think that a fellow pastor would be so vindictive." (Plagenz)

I often ask myself whether I would have made my opinions about entertainment evangelism public if I had anticipated the furor it would cause. Would I put myself in a position again where large numbers of Christians would try to discredit me? Most persons never truly enjoy criticism, and I identify with such discomfort.

In this book I am raising the same issues again. I firmly believe that—if we are going to talk about change—church leaders must capture the attention of their congregations and those who are seeking God.

I have another explanation for such anger in our churches. The real reason for much of the hostility is not for the reasons stated. Much of that bluster is a smoke screen for boredom and misplaced joy.

1 REJOICE ALWAYS

When I started in my ministry, I was quite naive. I expected that when a community of joy began to grow, the entire kingdom of God would rejoice that people were coming into a worshiping relationship with Jesus Christ. Congregations around us would celebrate.

The Bible talks about rejoicing with those who rejoice. "Rejoice in the Lord always; again I will say, Rejoice" (Phil. 4:4). I assumed that when we began rejoicing with large numbers of unchurched people, Lutherans and Christians everywhere would be pleased. Hardly! The more we grew, the more we were criticized for allegedly selling out the traditions of our fathers. The more evangelistic we became, the more leaders from around the church seemed to take aim at what we were doing. All of this fear and insecurity deeply puzzles me.

The Church Membership Initiative Study, sponsored by the Aid Association for Lutherans in 1993, began to illustrate what we are experiencing. We know that of all of the Lutheran congregations in the United States, only about 20 percent are growing. The rest are either stable or declining. Eighty percent of our congregations are not growing. We often hear about the 20/80 rule in organizations (which is sometimes called the Pareto principle): 20 percent of the people do 80 percent of the work, and 80 percent of the people do 20 percent of the work. Most church leaders know

that this principle is operative in individual congregations—
that about 20 percent of the congregation is deeply involved
in the core ministries of the organization. Perhaps the principle also applies to the denomination as a whole.

The various characteristics of growing and declining congregations are detailed. The growing 20 percent are open to
change, use a variety of programs and worship forms, and
have a strong sense of vision. Many of these change agencies
have also been the strongest supporters of our ministry at the
Community Church of Joy. Growing congregations are
thrilled when other churches are also growing.

One of the most basic characteristics of stable and declining churches is deep suspicion of growing churches. Many
of the stable and declining churches expend large sums of
energy and passion in attacking those congregations that are
growing. Growing churches by definition are in the midst of
changes in terms of restored lives, new structures, environ-
ments, and languages. These changes further threaten the
stability of those traditional things that define declining
churches.

Whenever I (or anyone from Joy) speak or write, I auto-
matically expect repercussions. Certainly the article on entertainment as a vehicle for evangelism triggered a visceral
reaction. But that issue, of course, cannot be separated from
the fact that, according to the Evangelical Lutheran Church
in America's development office records, Joy is the fastest-
growing Lutheran congregation in the United States.

The Mission of the Church: Make Disciples—Everywhere

The basic conviction of most evangelical Christians is that
the New Testament presumes the growth of the church. In
the Gospels and in Acts, we see that Jesus and the early
church want the church to grow, to reach the entire world

with the news that Christ is risen and that Jesus is Lord. The claim that three thousand persons were baptized at Pentecost speaks more forcefully about the power of the Spirit to transform lives than if only three had been baptized.

Pat Keifert (who studies growing churches) asked an assembled group of theologians, "Does the New Testament presume the growth of the church?" The question was met with hostility and avoidance. The profound ambivalence about the mission of established denominations creates the kind of climate where the energy of the elite is expended on denouncing or regulating innovations. What a waste of passion.

Twenty percent of our congregations are focused on the Great Commission—Christ's command that we reach out to new people. They see growth as part of the New Testament vision. Strategies for growth come out of that vision. Apparently far too many of the other 80 percent have turned inward, and large numbers may perish.

 KEY DISCOVERY: Empowering leadership produces growing congregations.

A feature article in the *Minnesota Monthly* tells about a similar phenomenon in the arts community. Three years prior to the article, the Ordway Theater in St. Paul hired a new director. He was told that his primary goal was to increase the audience, and he did just that. In just three years the subscriber base has grown from 3,300 to 31,000. During the past season over 650,000 people have attended live performances. In just three years the Ordway has gone from an enterprise always in the red to a successful entrepreneurial organization hosting popular entertainment.

The result, as might be expected, is that the rest of the arts community in the Twin Cities is apoplectic. One of the other arts leaders comments, "It's a devil's pact that the Ordway has set up. They have taken the artistic low road with such mainstream. I think we should be curators in this business and not just money producers" (Fox). In other words, if people actually enjoy the presentations and if they respond to entertaining music, then the programs must be artistic sellouts; the audience is stupid, and the art critic knows what is best.

This kind of elitism about music and art is remarkably similar to what many theologians think about pastors and even more so about the ignorant masses who worship with one another. We are selling out Jesus, because like "primitive savages" we prefer music and worship that resonate with our emotions.

Our critics often assert that they have been conditioned by artistic and musical tastes that have been formed and tested over centuries. In the case of Lutherans, this forming has been happening since the days of Bach and Beethoven. The critics assert that these standards of taste and behavior have been "handed down," and that it is their obligation to make sure that new disciples are formed by the same rules and practices in worship and preaching that were created during the Reformation.

But when we take a closer look at these standards of "high culture" and at how we came to acquire a pompous liturgy, we notice that all sorts of cultural influences were used and employed for the sake of the biblical mandate to bring the good news to *all* people. The music and philosophical ideas of the Renaissance were spread through printing presses and had an enormous effect on people *four hundred* years ago. By utilizing various media the church was able to dictate the spread of Christian culture.

Among the strongest forces that shape the tastes of elitist theologians are the Enlightenment theories of Immanuel Kant. Sociologist Tex Sample helps me understand that

> [this] form of elitist taste is not, of course, eternal. Immanuel Kant (1724–1804) developed one of the most sophisticated

arguments for this view of aesthetics in his *Critique of Judgment*. Kant proposes that art, or the aesthetic, should be understood as an end in itself. Its purpose is intrinsic. It is not a means to anything else—not ethical values or religion or hedonism. Kant says that it is "a purposeless purposefulness." Since its only purpose is aesthetic it serves no utilitarian aim, no matter how good it is and regardless of its makeup. (Sample, 29-30)

I think that this conflict is felt in our stable and declining churches when we advise them to "use" music and drama as a vehicle for evangelism. They forget that they have been using some type of music for four hundred years and that its use may or may not be effective in the current environment.

Words of support for the Ordway Theater's success came from the head of another enterprise, who said, "I see ourselves as working in a 'cultural ecosystem,' and the stronger the Ordway becomes, the stronger we can become. The stronger we become, the stronger others can be."

I believe that we live in a religious ecosystem. The stronger Community Church of Joy becomes, the stronger other congregations in our city and our denomination can become. Power is truly unlimited and flexible. When one congregation thrives, it empowers others. New disciples are sent forth.

Shared Power in the Spirit

Most congregations appear to think that power is limited. Growing congregations are seen, not as empowering, but as places that have sold their power to another cause. Where is the Holy Spirit in all of this? I believe that the Spirit gives all of us unlimited power. Whenever one congregation does well, it electrifies us with power and new life for the whole church.

KEY DISCOVERY: Entertainment wisely used with integrity is powerful and effective.

Perhaps part of the reason entertainment evangelism is often regarded with suspicion is that so much of what passes for Christian entertainment is deprived of integrity; that is, it is put to a false use. Cable television presents Christian entertainers who often seem to be caricatures of themselves. After the widely publicized debacles involving television evangelists such as Jim and Tammy Bakker and Jimmy Swaggart, it is hard to imagine forms of Christian entertainment that move us beyond charlatanry.

The tendency to disparage Christians as responsible for such images is widespread. James Wall, editor of *The Christian Century,* tells about an appearance he made at the University of Maryland, where he talked about the Christian faith as a motivating base for dialogue and action in the public sphere. What concerned him, he said, was not so much the media's failure to respect religion as an objective presence in the society, but its inability even to comprehend how religious faith as a subjective reality could be the driving force in the lives of individuals. Someone in the audience immediately (and predictably) brought up Jim Bakker and Jimmy Swaggart as the logical counterpoint to Wall's argument. Such a linkage of clergy misconduct with genuine religious claims has almost become automatic, Wall contends.

Any admiration of Christian entertainment suffers the same fate. Even mention the idea, and someone will throw the example of Bakker at you. Bring up the idea of trying to make worship more relevant and user-friendly, and listen as P. T. Barnum is brought into the conversation. Connect Christian practices with emotion, and get ready for a lecture about Elmer Gantry (the character in the 1927 novel by Lewis Sinclair).

The present culture is attuned to and even preoccupied with entertainment. Some social critics, such as Neil Postman, think that we in our culture are *Amusing Ourselves to Death*; and many of us probably are. Yet with so many messages competing for attention in our digital world, can we admit that the whole concept of entertainment in worship and evangelism might have some validity?

Entertainment in our culture is usually based on personality—a star's personality is so appealing that he or she is able to create a virtual relationship with large numbers of people. When this highly visible singer or actor falls, the potential for damaging the good news that he or she proclaimed is greater. The entertainer's behavior or character may not match his or her message, and this gap in integrity is of import to all visible Christian leaders. There is indeed more potential for scandal when we link a person such as a politician, an entertainer, or even a minister to the gospel witness and mission of the congregation. Perhaps the risks are outweighed by the benefits to God's kingdom. That risk/benefit factor we decide case by case as we look at the convenants that we make with one another in ministry. We examine our relationships, making a series of covenants with one another, so that the leadership of the congregation develops a process for testing and proving the character, competence, and maturity of its partners in ministry (see chapter 6).

I argue that there is such a thing as high-quality, substantial Christian entertainment that can deeply touch lives in ways that traditional approaches to ministry never could. That others have come to this realization seems to be supported by the fact that tens of thousands of congregations in established denominations are now choosing to experiment with worship styles. A *Wall Street Journal* article says that *1,500 Lutheran congregations have started alternative worship services in the previous three years* (Niebuhr). Congregations all over the country are trying to find some kind of balance between old and new, tradition and novelty.

Entertainment has certainly become a watchword, a shibboleth, for those who wish to maintain the status quo. Perhaps a better word might be discovered at another time and place. Perhaps Pat Keifert's phrase "welcoming the stranger" is a better way of talking about user-friendly churches.

 KEY DISCOVERY: "Old theology" + "new music" = effective evangelism.

Loren Mead, in *The Once and Future Church*, contends that when we are confronted by incessant change, denial is one of the most common responses. We tend to deny that which we do not want to accept. Part of denial is often an attempt to destroy or discredit the messenger who brings the bad news.

While I was speaking at a senior pastors' conference at Valparaiso University, someone asked me, "Kallestad, why do so many people dislike you so much?" My response was, "You tell me."

Another responded, "What you are saying means that all that we have learned and been trying to do for a lifetime needs to be changed. We are not willing to do that."

This fear of change reminds me of a college professor I know who is retiring early. I asked him why he was not choosing to continue teaching until the mandatory retirement age. His answer was insightful: "In order to teach today's college students, I would have to completely retool. I am not willing to do that at my age."

Denial, as well as refusal to attempt change, is widespread. Some of this denial surged toward me recently when I received a newsletter from a nearby church. In the pastor's column there was a blistering attack on entertainment evangelism. The pastor hinted that he and his fellow leaders were far too sophisticated and theologically astute to sink to such pedestrian levels. Later in the same newsletter was a half-page announcement about an upcoming Sunday. A well-known bluegrass music group would be leading all three worship services. Bluegrass music! Isn't that entertainment? I was tempted to send my neighbor a note that congratulated him for experimenting with entertainment evangelism, but why should I pick a fight with someone who agrees with me in practice?

Ever since I was a part of the gospel team movement in college I have seen how entertaining music and worship are not antithetical to effective worship. New forms can often enhance worship. Different styles attract different groups of people. In fact, some studies today suggest that more and more people are choosing a church more because of its style of worship than because of its theology or heritage. The style of worship, the language, the music, the preaching, the programs—all have at least as much influence on people's choice of a particular church as the substance has. While there is something to be feared in this shift, it is yet another change on which we do not have a vote.

If the church is to be viable in the twenty-first century, we have no choice but to find new styles and forms for communicating the gospel. We need to find new bridges between the gospel and the secular mind-set. Entertainment can be one of those bridges, but it is certainly not the only one.

Futurist Joel Barker, in his book on paradigms, presents a telling story about the watchmakers of Switzerland. Early in the 1960s the Swiss were the premier creators of watches in the world. They had nearly 90 percent of the market share. During the mid-1960s one of the Swiss watchmakers invented a new style of watch. It was the quartz model, one thousand times more accurate than the old mechanical watches. Not surprisingly, the Swiss watchmakers rejected the new innovation. They asserted that they were creating products that were as good as could possibly be made. Why change? So they ignored the new method for measuring time.

Some Japanese watchmakers took the model back to Japan and developed it. As the cliché goes, "the rest is history." Today the Japanese have nearly 90 percent of the market share for watches, and the Swiss have less than 10 percent. Reflecting on this turn of events, Joel Barker makes a rather haunting statement—one that I think has implications for the church: "When a paradigm shifts, then everything goes back to zero" (Barker 1992, 15-16).

Established congregations have had for the most part an effective tenure over the past two hundred years in North America. Such staples as outstanding classical music, exemplary sixteenth-century Elizabethan language, and a traditional understanding of theology have characterized this church. Today's reality, however, is that the amount of people responding positively to denominationalism and mainstream congregations is dropping, in some cases very sharply.

We have, in the last quarter of the twentieth century, lost almost an entire generation of young adults, who regard the church as irrelevant. We are in serious danger of losing the next generation as well.

 KEY DISCOVERY: Innovation produces more refreshment than ice cream.

For the Community Church of Joy, focusing on entertainment means connecting with people by showing hospitality, receiving and caring for guests, as well as capturing and holding people's attention. This concept is highlighted by the Ben and Jerry's Ice Cream factory in Vermont. In *Coloring Outside the Lines*, John Westfall links the philosophy of the ice cream company to that of the church.

On our last day in New England, we stopped for the tour of the Ben and Jerry's Ice Cream factory. We heard the fascinating story of Ben and Jerry, two college dropouts who sent away for a five-dollar mail order course on how to make ice cream. After only a few short years they were the third largest producers of gourmet ice cream in the world.

As their company grew, it became apparent to the two partners that their jobs had ceased to be fun. Work and its ensuing responsibilities were robbing them of their zest and creativity. According to the tour guide, they began to assess their company and determined that they were not in business to sell ice cream but to create joy.

Realizing their purpose, they hired a person to serve as Director of Joy for the company. The job consisted of fun activities and celebrations for the company and the community. Large stereo speakers were mounted in the factory so that loud party rock and roll would blare over the assembly lines. Believing that they were in the joy business, they set aside 7½ percent of pretax profits for charities, festivals, community service, and special causes. . . .

If Joy is our product, we are free to find new, creative ways to serve and encourage one another. When the stock market plummeted on Black Monday, panic and desperation were everywhere. Ben and Jerry were on the sidewalks of Wall Street scooping out free bowls of "economic crunch" ice cream. (Westfall, 100-101)

Maybe Christians can learn something from these two ice cream producers. We so often miss the joy. We have tended to act like quality control advisers for one another, rather than looking for a new, lighter yoke of joy. The old, heavy one doesn't work anymore. Besides, joy is what the yoke of Jesus Christ is all about: "My yoke is easy, and my burden is light" (Matt. 11:30).

Entertainment evangelism is not the message. It is not the gospel. It is by itself only a medium, which is not very much at all, but in this day of accelerating entertainment we can use this medium to proclaim the gospel in a new way. Forms always change, but the central truth of Jesus stays the same.

Imagineering, the art and process of seeing the same thing in a new way, means unearthing new and innovative ways to worship and reach out to the unchurched. Entertainment can be one of these. Imagine two pastors with clerical collars who are sitting in the midst of a crowd of people. The crowd is cheering and shouting. One cleric says to the other, "I hate football, but I love to be where people are excited about something" (from a cartoon by Larry Thomas). *Why not let the church be that place where people have joy?*

 KEY DISCOVERY: Welcome change as you would a great friend.

> *I am about to do a new thing;*
> *now it springs forth, do you not perceive it?*
> —Isaiah 43:19

A generation ago the roles of the pastoral leader and the elected leadership were abundantly clear. Leaders were above all to preserve and protect the heritage and pass on the traditions and rituals to the next generations. Leaders were empowered to stand against any threats that might buffet the congregation or the society. They were to be immovable forces against the winds of darkness and unbelief. Given the role of protectors of the faith, many leaders inevitably regarded change as a major threat. Change would lead to chaos and unpredictability. Once the cork is out of the bottle, there is no telling what might happen to the pure wine.

In Christendom, where everybody was somehow connected to the church, this kind of rearguard action was understandable. Sometimes it even worked for a time. This defensive stance became the primary operating principle of ministry for many clergy. However, in this world of post-

Christendom, where most people are not connected to the church, such an attitude is no longer plausible.

Change has come to our world suddenly, with hurricane-force winds. The entire landscape has been rearranged, and a different world is emerging. Just in case we think that there might be some respite from incessant change, futurists are now predicting that there will be more change in the last decade of this millennium than in the past three decades combined. Having seen a decade that opened with the Berlin Wall crumbling and ended with the Iron Curtain now transparent before our eyes, the advent of even more change will hardly surprise us.

Lyle Schaller says that there are only two constants in this world: Christ and change. In a very real sense, I believe that I was uniquely prepared to face accelerating change. My early childhood, my college days, my years of working with music, youth, and evangelism at Prince of Peace Lutheran Church, my seminary experience (especially my internship), and then my first year at Joy all were dominated by a common theme: *change.*

I virtually had no choice. I had to either adjust to change or give up. I had to either make change or go through life in a reactive frame of mind. Change was a given. The sooner I accepted that fact, the more prepared I would be for my call to lead.

Imagineering, a word made by combining *imagination* and *engineering,* refers to a way of anticipating change, imagining a new vision for a new day, and devising a strategy for implementing the new vision.

Urban and Rural Shifts

One of the most dramatic shifts that has taken place in America in the past generation has been the move from rural to urban. I am especially tuned in to this change because I experienced it personally. George Hunter notes that as this century began, only 10 to 20 percent of all Americans lived in urban areas. The rest were rural peoples. As the twentieth century rushes toward completion, the numbers have been reversed. Now 80 to 90 percent of Americans live in urban areas. Less than 20 percent are rural. This is a change of monumental proportions. George Hunter, in *How to Reach Secular People*, asserts that formerly mainline Protestant churches did not do well in urban ministry. Many church leaders look at the city as an evil place, far less receptive to the gospel than is the rural community.

Urban people have different perspectives than many rural residents. By and large, they accept and even celebrate change. Some may long for a more pastoral setting, perhaps even purchase a second home, or become weekend campers. Most of the time they embrace the dynamics of change. Urbanites expect to be faced with alternatives and given options. They shop at large malls rather than at general stores. This is the reason McDonald's, Burger King, Hardee's, and Wendy's often build right across from one another. Giving people more options is seen as good for business. Paired with this is the increasing mobility of urban dwellers. They will drive long distances to find what they want—to seek out options.

Urbanites gravitate toward institutions that offer options as well. Most urban people prefer larger institutions over smaller ones. They attend larger schools, cheer at larger stadiums, work at larger companies. Again, many people pine for the day when life was less complex, when small was beautiful. In the city, however, a critical mass is required even to survive. Sufficient size also affords the church capability for offering these options.

Observation tells us that most churched people in urban centers prefer larger congregations. Of all the major movements in Christianity in the past half-century, this is perhaps the most prominent. Hundreds, perhaps thousands of urban churches have become very large. Some are called mega-churches. These congregations are truly focusing on urban preferences, offering a wide range of programs, worship styles, and ministry options. My own sense is that congregations will continue to grow larger.

To counteract the perceived unfriendliness that is often associated with bigness, most large churches are creating many churches within the church. We call them small groups. The larger a church grows, the smaller it must become. Evaluating the changing attitudes of our culture always influences the way we do ministry.

Perhaps the change that will prove to be the most revolutionary in this period of time is that of the increasing impact of technology. For those of us who grew up in a time when the typewriter and the telephone were considered high-tech, this electronic revolution has seemed overwhelming. With the advent of fiber optics, information of all kinds—words, images, voices—races along electronic superhighways at the speed of light. Consumers will soon be able to have a small pie-plate-size dish mounted outside their homes and receive five hundred television channels. A small box in our living room will allow us to order any program we wish, when we want it. We will be able to shop for virtually any product from our home and even check our bank balances to see if we can afford what we are purchasing. A two-way link of video, audio, and other types of data is just around the corner. The possibilities are endless.

Of course, this fascination with technology does not address the basic human need for contact with other human beings, a search that must be centered in relationships. What gives purpose to human existence are relationships—with God, with ourselves, with others, and with the world itself. Despite all its capabilities, technology cannot provide us with these relationships. In fact, technology has the potential to isolate people.

Instead of helping people become part of the community, technology can accelerate the tendency of people to cocoon. They enter into the inner sanctum of their elaborate entertainment centers, lock their doors, and only interact with technology. If community is basic to human fulfillment, then technology can be more a part of the problem than of the solution.

Change is accelerating. We may not like all of the changes, but we do not get to vote on most of them. The leaders in this time of history need to look at change as a friend—to see change as providing new opportunities for the future. Every change is a possibility for ministry. Every shift opens new doors for innovation and creativity. *Responding proactively to change is the key to leadership as we enter the twenty-first century.*

At Joy we have attempted to understand as best we can the culture all around us and to make friends with the changes. We have then used our imagineering skills to work on how new opportunities might be created, how we might create new paradigms for ministry. Change for us is not a threat but a window of opportunity.

 KEY DISCOVERY: Learn from our failures.

Failure is not fatal, but the failure to change might be.
—John Wooden

People are afraid of change and try to keep change from happening. This has been a phenomenon in every generation. An important letter in American history highlights for me the fear and resistance toward change that I often encounter. Martin Van Buren, governor of New York at the time, wrote to President Andrew Jackson in the 1820s:

> The canal system of this country is being threatened by the spread of a new form of transportation known as "railroads." The federal government must preserve the canals for the following reasons:

1. If the canal boats are supplanted by railroads, serious unemployment will result. Captains, cooks, drivers, hostlers, repairmen, and lock tenders will be left without means of livelihood, not to mention the numerous farmers now employed in growing hay for the horses.

2. Boat builders would suffer and decline, whip and harness makers would be left destitute.

3. Canal boats are absolutely essential to the defense of the United States. In the event of unexpected trouble with England, the Erie Canal would be the only means by which we could ever move the supplies so vital to waging modern war.

As you know, Mr. President, railroad carriages are pulled at the enormous speed of fifteen miles per hour by engines which, in addition to endangering life and limb of passengers, roar and snort their way throughout the countryside, setting fire to crops, scaring livestock and frightening women and children. The Almighty certainly never intended that people should travel at such breakneck speed. (Quoted in Leith Anderson 1990, 169-70)

Each generation fears the next "railroad" and seeks to hold on to its version of "canal boats"—for good reason. Maybe we would all be better off if we still only had canal boats. We might be much safer if we were restricted to traveling fifteen miles per hour. Yet I sense that national security was not severely damaged when whip makers and hostlers were put out of business. We seem to have adjusted to this shock to the economy. Change comes whether we welcome it or not. Why not make change our friend?

Will Rogers once said that a person who can only see a week ahead is always popular. Such a person reflects the views of society. Looking into a rearview mirror is not threatening, but the person who looks a year or more ahead is looking through a telescope.

I have always attempted to view the world and the future through a telescope. Sometimes it has been difficult to interpret what I have seen. I am the first to admit that articulating a vision of the future is not easy. To convince people that what is seen in the telescope can be reality and not just fantasy is an ongoing and sobering task.

One of our church members put this into perspective. "Insanity," he said, "is doing the same thing over and over and expecting different results." Many new initiatives fail. Those who consistently question whether something new will work are often correct. But when we see clearly the changes that are coming, when we create something that captures the imagination of our people in response to those changes, then we can change the world.

The role of a leader is to be constantly looking into the telescope to catch a glimpse of the changes that are coming. Imagineering creates a vision of how to respond to change, how to re-create the ministry and expand our vision. When our vision connects with the specific change happening in our culture, we can truly have an "aha" occurrence.

Imagineering

"Reengineering the Corporation," an article in *USA Today* (November 8, 1993) by John Hillkirk, describes the situation of the 655 people who design, illustrate, and write Hallmark's greeting cards. Today these people have very enjoyable careers, but not long ago many Hallmark employees needed get-well cards because of low morale.

Hallmark previously created greeting cards in a step-by-step process that mimicked one of Henry Ford's assembly lines. Artists and writers rarely spoke. Employees who created the fancy calligraphy worked in a building a quarter of a mile away. Because of delays and rework, it took Hallmark more than twenty-four months to create and produce a card. But fortunately for the employees, the old process is now just another Hallmark memory. The privately owned card maker has reengineered. That means it has radically redesigned its card-creation process. Today, artists and writers work together in interactive, creative teams. Their bright, colorful offices are designed to stimulate creativity and the flow of ideas.

Hillkirk writes that reengineering is one of the hottest concepts in management today. Dozens of large companies are reengineering all or part of their operations. Reengineering means basically wiping the slate clean and asking, "If we could start all over again, what would we do differently? What would we eliminate entirely? What can we do that would make things easier for our customers?"

Imagineering is truly similar to reengineering, except that imagination affects all areas, not just the bottom line. Our task as church leaders is not so much to create something that works but to envision creatively what God wants us to do. We wish to image and imagine what God wants us to be. Imagineering means rediscovering our theological imaginations.

I have learned over the years that *failure is never final.* Strange as it may seen, failure has often been my friend. It gives me important and essential insight on how to act the next time. *For me the greatest failure in the world is the failure to act on new ideas.*

Ideas are some of God's greatest gifts. Ideas should be approached like rare and priceless jewels. I constantly attend seminars, read books, and meet with outstanding leaders so that I might discover a new idea or two. Leaders are learners. When we stop learning, we can no longer lead.

So much creative innovation is avoided because we tend to be afraid of what others might think or say. We fear and resist change because we know we might become the laughing stocks of yesterday's crowd. I know these feelings personally. I am also realistic enough to know that unrelenting criticism of change will continue in the future. Even though I have come to expect criticism, and even to dismiss much of it, I must admit that it still does sting. Undeserved condemnation is always painful, but I am fortunate in that whenever I am facing the arrows of attack, I always have the option of remembering my cousin Mary.

Mary was born with some physical deformities. She has a twisted nose, gnarled teeth, a misshapen lip, and speaks with an impediment. She was laughed at and humiliated by her peers from her earliest childhood. Mary would usually stand at the back of the crowd or sit in the back of the room because she was so ashamed.

One day her grade school teacher changed her life—her very self-image. Mary's teacher came to her desk, got down on her knees and looked Mary straight in the eye. "Mary," she said, "I wish you were my little girl."

This teacher was the most loved and adored teacher in the entire school, and here she was telling Mary how she valued her, how she wished Mary belonged to her. From that moment Mary saw herself as someone who was special. She felt loved, appreciated, and accepted. Today Mary lives out that kind of self-image. She is loving, self-assured, positive, and successful.

When I am faced with criticism, I am constantly reminded that Jesus Christ also comes to each of us face-to-face and says, "You are mine, and I am delighted." If God believes I am somebody, I must have infinite worth. When I look at myself through God's eyes, my fear is replaced by a confident, courageous faith.

Calvary Lutheran Church in Golden Valley, Minnesota, has a mission statement that includes the following: "Calvary is a place where Jesus Christ is Lord and everybody is somebody." The psalmist tells us that each of us is the "apple of [God's] eye." We were created in the image of God, crowned with glory and honor (Pss. 17:8; 8:5). When others disvalue me, I remember that God always sees me as valuable.

Peter Drucker, in his book *Innovation and Entrepreneurship*, tells us that every practice rests on a theory, even if those carrying out the practice are not aware of the theory or are looking for the theory to support the practice. He says that entrepreneurship rests on the theory that change is normal and, indeed, healthy. The best way to lead in this kind of a world is through discovering ways to see change as an opportunity. Drucker says that the major task of leadership today is to do something in a different way rather than just trying to do better what is already being done.

Most change comes whether we want it or not. We do not get a vote. Change is accelerating with each decade. As we face choices that will help us in the midst of change, the status quo is not an option. We grow or we die. We change or we atrophy. I have made change, my friend. I see change as an opportunity.

Vision is about change. Imagineering is about change. Life is about change.

 KEY DISCOVERY: Self-definition is integral to effecting significant change.

One of the most important changes that I made early in my years at Joy was the decision to define myself. *I created my own personal mission statement.* In order for me to be a leader, I needed to decide what I was called to do and also what I should not do. There always remain only so many hours in the week, and I have only so much energy. My task was to focus on that which was essential.

I realized that most of my first year had been spent reacting. I was running myself ragged, responding to every brushfire that was breaking out. My energy was constantly consumed by dysfunctional and contrary people. Some of the elected leadership saw me primarily as a "gofer," a person to react to their whim and call. They did not want a leader; they wanted a chaplain, if not a doormat. They believed I was called to do all of the ministry. They defined their role as making sure I did it.

I decided—not a bit too early—that this would not work. If we were going to become an urban congregation with multiple ministries, most definitely this would not work. I had not read Edwin Friedman's classic book, *Generation to Generation*, at that time, but I already felt and knew within what he would later explain on theoretical grounds.

Friedman asserts that there are two kinds of leaders who generally rise in the church. One is a charismatic leader, and the other is a consensus leader. The former leads by the power and influence of his or her vision or personality; the latter leads by the will of the people. Charismatic leaders tend to be more dynamic and creative; consensus leaders tend to be more behind-the-scenes. I defined myself as a charismatic leader.

Friedman goes on to say that from a family-systems point of view, two problems are endemic to both charismatic and consensus leaders. Both types of leaders give too much power to dependent people, and both types tend to over-function. It is inherent in the family system.

Both types of leaders spend far too much time reacting to the loudest voices, the extremists, the screamers, the dysfunctional troublemakers. This causes them much turmoil. They get up earlier and go home later. In other words, these leaders take on the pathology of those who oppose them, and they become unhealthy.

What Friedman suggests is that *true leaders need to differentiate themselves from others and stay in touch.* To differentiate oneself is to discover and affirm one's own gifts. A leader seeks to understand what God is calling the leader to be. This understanding helps a leader establish boundaries. All leaders learn quickly that if we do not define ourselves, someone else is sure to do it for us.

A leader also stays in touch. With whom? We stay in touch with those who need to embrace our self-definition. That could be the elected leadership, or it could be some unofficial leaders, or it could be both. A leader quickly learns with whom to stay in touch.

When I wrote my personal mission statement, when I defined myself, everything changed. I began with the vision and focused my energy in that direction. I decided not to spend much time at all reacting to dependent people. I even recommended to some of the loudest voices of opposition that they find other congregations.

I set more and more time aside each week to focus on the vision. I refused to spend time on pathology. I went out and found other leaders who could share in our vision, and I enlisted them in the leadership. *I became vision-centered rather than problem-centered.* My ministry was transformed.

We have made many mistakes. We hired some new staff members too quickly, and they provided more problems than solutions. We had to go through a rapid learning curve on hiring. Sometimes we went too far out on a limb in terms of financial commitments. We ended up being squeezed.

At other times we did not communicate as well as we might have with the entire congregation. (Lyle Schaller calls this "redundant communication," which means overcommunicating in an age in which there is already much competition for the attention of our listeners.) We have sometimes reaped confusion or unnecessary resistance because of sloppy communication.

Although we didn't fine-tune our strategies as well as we should have, we have never lost sight of our vision. I spend almost no time reacting to people who do not share our vision. I am proactively concentrating on the vision. I spend less time in the office than most pastors. I take Mondays off and spend them with Mary. I take Fridays and use this time to imagine and dream about what might be. I have few evening meetings. I have learned how to define myself and stay in touch.

Without a vision the people perish. With action a vision can even be transcended. We reached our goal of three thousand members long before the year 1990. Our staff plan was implemented and even expanded beyond projections. Our budget went well over $1 million long before our plan suggested.

Robert Schuller had asked me many years earlier, "Walt, do you believe in miracles?" My answer has only become a clearer "Of course!" Amazing miracles, far beyond our fondest expectations, have taken place. With God all things are possible.

We moved consistently over a period of seventeen years toward reaching our compelling vision of all people knowing Jesus Christ and becoming responsible members of his church. We have consistently tried to share Christ's love with joy, inspired by the Holy Spirit. With vision the people live.

▼ LIST YOUR KEY DISCOVERIES ▼

What are your key discoveries about yourself and the ministry of your church after reading about imagineering, entertainment evangelism, and elitism? How would you describe the aesthetic tastes of the people at your church?

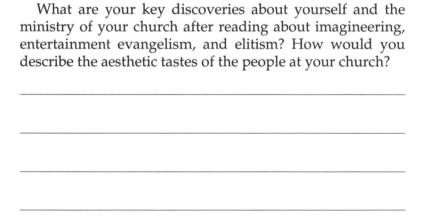

CHAPTER 2 A VISION: A STRATEGY AND A PURPOSE

A vision stirred within me. A dream had been building in me for several years, and I wanted more than anything else to establish that dream at Community Church of Joy. I imagined a congregation that would grow to a point where it could be a powerful witness to Jesus Christ all over the northwest corner of Phoenix. The vision evoked images of the people who do not go to church.

I wanted to help shape a congregation that would develop revolutionary new ways of reaching out to strangers—of showing hospitality. I imagined myself participating in a wide-ranging variety of new forms of worship and music. My vision was of an oasis in the middle of the desert. I saw living waters flowing in the midst of a parched field.

 KEY DISCOVERY: The greater the vision, the greater the struggle.

Angry antagonists hit me early at Joy. On my very first Sunday in the pulpit, a member walked out of church and asked me what would become a pivotal question. "Pastor Kallestad, whose side are you on?" What a shock! Whose side are you on? I was dumbfounded by the question. My first, rather flippant answer was, "I am on God's side."

I soon learned that the question was anything but frivolous. The people were deadly serious. My future very likely

Helpless Flashback

I want to plug my ears, to pull a pillow down over my head and blot out all the painful sounds. Loud and angry voices turn into shouts. Increasingly shrill attacks reverberate throughout the rooms of the parsonage home where I am growing up as a young child.

The sobs of my mother in an adjoining room are tearing me apart, sobs that seem to arise from the very core of her being. I cower in the face of the abuse being hurled, like sharpened arrows, at the wounded person of my father, the pastor.

I feel an urge deep inside to rush into that room and chase the intruders away. I want to rise up to my ten-year-old tallest and defend my beleaguered father. With every fiber of my being I want to tell the whole world that my depended on how I answered that question. Whose side would I be on? Two very distinct sides made themselves visible almost immediately. One was "for" and one was "against."

Those who were "for" were positive toward most everything, even change. They had called me as the pastor. They were pushing for the positive energy that creates a vision, for reaching out to new people. Those who were "against" did not want to call me. They certainly did not want any kind of innovation or change. Suspicion and a negative spirit marked their comments and their body language.

I discovered that these two groups had absolutely no ability to communicate with each other. Dialogue was impossible. A classic power struggle was evident from the beginning of my ministry. Intimidation and innuendo were the weapons of choice.

The first meetings of the church council after I arrived should have been videotaped. They could be used as case studies in seminary laboratories. I have never seen anything quite like these struggles. The only thing comparable is the memory of my father being assaulted by the leaders of the congregation in rural Minnesota, or some of the clinical meetings I was a part of during my ministry internship.

Arguments became highly personal. People shouting at one another was commonplace. A split right down the middle was obvious. The treasurer, the one who threatened not to pay me, was among the most hostile and negative people I have ever met. At one meeting he shouted at me, "Kallestad, every time you open your mouth, you cost us money." At another meeting he became so upset that he knocked a table over, sending the financial papers all over the floor. He then stomped out of the meeting, nearly ripping the door off its hinges.

Prior to my arrival at Joy, the church council had tried to address the money crunch by contracting with a private childcare enterprise to use our facilities. This was no small matter. In exchange for $11,000 a year, we were giving this program every square inch of our space for six days a week, twelve hours a day.

Our facility had little capacity to handle this kind of use. I was called repeatedly to be a troubleshooter—to unstop clogged toilets and mop up around leaking faucets and sinks. Children paraded through my office on a regular basis, climbing all over my desk. We could plan no program or ministry during the week, for the

dad has been called by God to be a pastor, a shepherd, and a servant. But he was never called to be a doormat.

Nobody has the right to abuse a pastor this way. Especially when this pastor happens to be my father. But what can I do? I'm only ten. All that is available to me is to feel the deep pain and humiliation of the moment and to store these feelings deep inside of me.

The climax of the evening is not long in coming. I hear one of the loudest, most insistent voices shout with rising passion, "Walther, I am going to ask for your resignation."

I feel utterly hopeless and despondent. My feelings are not only for my father but also for my mother and my three older sisters. I know instinctively that this means still another move. We have moved often already.

Now, once again, I will be uprooted from a home I have come to love and from friendships and community. Being forced to start all over again somewhere else is not fair. I do not want to go. I have just become familiar with this environment, and now we have to leave.

space was completely filled. The biggest shock came when I learned that the council had signed a ten-year contract with the childcare directors.

To compound an already serious financial problem, I found a letter from the national church on my desk the day I arrived. The note demanded immediate payment on the loan that had been extended to Joy some years earlier for the purchase of the land. At that time, the denomination had demonstrated remarkable vision by purchasing ten acres of land for this new congregation.

Now they were insisting that we sell five of those acres so that we might pay off the debt. As might be expected, the council was polarized. As far as I was concerned, this was a "no-brainer." The land was our future. We should never get rid of any of our land. We would need more land in the future, not less. *Never sell the land.*

Robert Schuller once told me, "There is much more of the future in the land than in the leader." When so many congregations were desperate for more land, we would have been destroying our future had we accommodated the request. Instead, we sold $272,000 worth of bonds and paid for the land.

Many days I felt that leading this struggling little congregation was like trying to push water uphill. We had a marginal site and very poor visibility. We had enough acres, but now were being pushed to sell half of it. We had an inadequate facility that was being overused by a childcare program with what seemed to be a lifetime contract. We had a divided church and a dysfunctional church council. Our primary mission that first year was survival. Success in that mission was by no means assured.

We had already turned inward. As a church that was only three years old, we had moved very quickly from being a mission to being a maintenance organization. The whole climate was one of suspicion and defeat.

Not long after I arrived I began to hear rumors. Meetings were being called with the expressed purpose of sending me packing. A significant number of people in the church wanted me to leave. Incredible! I had just arrived, I had hardly unpacked, and now they wanted me to go.

All of those old memories of my father being pushed out of that rural Minnesota church came flooding back into my consciousness. I had only been ten years old, but it seemed like yesterday. Was my fate to be the same? I might not even last my first year. Had I made a terrible mistake by accepting this call? Was I in the right profession?

At about this time I received a phone call from the congregation we had attended when I was on internship in the panhandle of Texas, asking if I would consider a call to be senior pastor. In spite of all of the heartache, I still felt called to Joy.

 KEY DISCOVERY: A vision is most effectively shaped with love.

I was desperate. I searched diligently for answers. For some years I had sought in my ministry to learn from Lloyd Ogilvie of Hollywood Presbyterian Church. When I received some information about a seminar he was leading, I immediately signed up. I arranged to spend some time with Ogilvie personally.

I unloaded for him the story of how I had come to this struggling little church in northwest Phoenix and how I was in danger of being fired. I wept throughout much of the conversation. The depth of my consternation was not difficult to see. I learned again what I already knew: Most church leaders understand all about pain and heartache. Lloyd Ogilvie was no exception. He had walked down similar paths and could empathize with me.

At the end of our conversation, he said to me, "Walt, I am not sure what you should do. Let me recommend one focus. When you go back to Joy, *do everything you can to show people how much God loves them.* Give people a hug when they come to church. Hug them when they leave the church. Hug everyone. Do all that you can to create a climate of love in your congregation. Love can be contagious."

His words did not strike a very responsive chord in me. I grew up as a Norwegian in Minnesota. Reticence about displays of affection and a lack of communication were a way of life. Our family never hugged at all, especially my father. Often on Saturday nights we would join the throngs on Main Street in our town. If we saw any couples brave enough to show even the most innocent kinds of affection, my parents would express their disgust.

Thus I knew little about a climate of affection. I was not much of a hugger, and I was not thrilled with Ogilvie's suggestion. I was especially averse to hugging some of those people at Joy. But I was desperate. I knew that Ogilvie had been around much longer than I had, so I felt I should at least try his idea.

The first Sunday after the workshop provided the opportunity. I was determined to hug everyone in sight. I sensed that I would be tested early. Sure enough, the first person who walked out of church after the service was the treasurer.

Of all people, he was the one most hostile toward me on the church council, and he was the leader of those who were trying to speed my departure.

He was stomping and snorting like a large bull as he was leaving. There was nothing unusual about such behavior for him. But I abandoned all caution and threw my arms around him, giving him a big hug. I thought for a moment that he was going to hit me. He rushed out into the parking lot, jumped in his car, and with tires squealing he raced away. I never saw him again.

Frank Harrington says that "Every church should have a membership drive every once in a while, [which is] a process to drive out all of the troublemakers." I wonder if this is what he means.

I continued to hug, hoping to increase a climate of welcoming and hospitality. Of course the word spread quickly throughout the "against" group in the congregation that "Kallestad is crazy, unbalanced, out of control." So much for love, I was thinking.

Meetings in which the major business item was getting rid of me continued. As a rookie pastor, I kept giving those who opposed me ammunition. On one of my first Sundays at Joy I saw an altar cloth draped on the Communion cup. I removed it during the Communion service, innocently crumpled it, and put it aside. I had no inkling that the church had developed a practice of folding the cloth in a certain way and placing it in a special, designated spot. Perhaps I was absent on the day that the seminary taught us about folding altar cloths. The leader of the altar guild cornered me with fire in her eyes as soon as the worship service was over. One-by-one, I seemed to be moving people into the "against" camp. I ascertained that at the rate I was driving people away, I would soon be able to offer seminars on church decline.

Focusing the Original Vision

Annual church meetings often become forums for the most strident and hostile forces to defend and keep the status quo. Some feedback process needs to be in place, but the annual meeting is an idea whose time has gone.

Our first annual meeting was a classic donnybrook. We should have videotaped that event too. No soap opera has ever had such drama: four hours of uninterrupted vitriol and bitterness. All of this was happening at a church called Joy. I left for home after the meeting and vomited. I was so traumatized that I was sick for several days. My energy level had dropped to almost zero.

A short time later I received a call from the local fire department. The caller informed me that our church building was burning. My first thought as I heard the news was to let it burn. That might be the answer. Burn, baby, burn. I felt as if I could then depart with some dignity.

However, as I drove toward the church, suddenly a wave of sorrow came over me. I started to cry. I felt like such a failure. I prayed out loud, "God, if you want me to leave, I will leave. If you want me to leave the ministry, I will follow your will."

 KEY DISCOVERY: A vision of God's decision is a vision with God's provision.

"But if you want me to stay here," I continued, "then you are going to have to help me. If you want me to remain a pastor, then you must use your power. I cannot do this alone." I was almost overwhelmed with a sense of sorrow. What an irony! I was the one who had never wanted to be a pastor. I had wanted to avoid any situation where I could suffer the same fate as my father. How had I ended up here?

Fortunately, the fire was quickly contained. It caused only minor damage. However, God had fanned a fire in my heart that has never gone out.

The statistical report for the first year was not encouraging. We had managed to downsize our membership from two hundred to one hundred. At the rate we were going, by one year later we would most likely be one-half as large again. If that were to have happened, then we could have just shut the doors and walked away. Hardly anyone would have noticed.

Shortly after the annual meeting, I knew it was time either to become proactive or to leave. We had one member of the council who delighted in parking in the space reserved for the pastor. Also, he came and sat at my desk and went through my mail, often opening letters. I asked him to quit this kind of intrusive behavior, but he ignored me. When I asked him why he continued to do such things, his answer was instructive: "I was here before you were here, and I will be here after you are gone."

Finally I could not stand his behavior any longer, and, in what turned out to be a defining moment, I shouted at him, "I am the pastor of this church and you are not. If you ever park in my spot again, I will have your car towed away. If you ever go through my mail again, I will have you arrested."

I was at the end of my rope. Lloyd Ogilvie had counseled me to pray that antagonistic people be either removed or revived. My expertise seemed at this point to be in the removal mode.

I learned during that first year what many other new pastors have discovered: To turn around a church is one of the most difficult and draining challenges possible. When a church is sick, healing is all that works. Many of us do not have the particular gifts it takes to heal an ailing church. It would be far easier and much less costly to close down many declining congregations and create new ones. Many of those new congregations could even be started in the same buildings as the old ones.

I was inclined to think that nearly anyone who would have accepted the call to Joy would have met similar resistance as I did. Some may have had more experience than I had in dealing with the various pathologies of antagonistic church members, yet I had not come totally unprepared. I had been through some incredibly wrenching and difficult periods earlier. I became convinced that these dark periods of my life truly had prepared me for the first year at Joy.

As we wrote the annual reviews of my first year, it was clear to me that we did not have much time left. The church council was split. Arguments lasted well into the night over any and every mundane or irrelevant detail one could imagine. I became sick before most meetings. If I managed to avoid premeeting sickness, the meeting itself would make me sick.

I discovered that constant conflict wears down a person. My resistance was at rock bottom. Usually this is a point where someone either crashes or leaves. I was determined to do neither. I wanted to lead. I needed to direct all my talents and abilities and experiences in the direction of leadership. I was called to lead Joy from gridlock to mission. Vision casting was the answer.

 KEY DISCOVERY: Shift leaders from operating out of present reality to operating out of vision.

> *Where there is no vision, the people perish.*
> —Proverbs 29:18 KJV

At the beginning of my second year at Community Church of Joy, I recommended that we change our focus. We had been concentrating primarily on problems. Now we needed to look at possibilities. In other words, *we needed to create a vision.* We needed a clear and inspiring vision that would pull us toward the future.

Without a vision we had no idea of where we were going. We had no inkling whatsoever of when we might get there. The writer of Proverbs gave us our theme, "Where there is no vision, the people perish." We knew this in our very bones. We had no vision, and we were indeed perishing. It was time for a brand-new direction.

The original vision of Joy was similar to that of most established Protestant churches. That original vision statement went something like this:

> We want to have an open door for all active Lutherans who might move into the community. We share that vision with countless other congregations. If we honor the traditions of our predecessors, then those people who have grown up Lutheran will continue to join our membership.

We remember the days or at least hear stories about the time when boats filled with Scandinavians and Germans flocked to this country. Lutheran churches were filled by immigrants who were colonizing a new world as resident aliens. However, even in the glory days for Lutheran expansion and colonization, very few of these people from overseas came to colonize Phoenix. Such boats no longer come. If any immigrants are coming today into Phoenix or elsewhere, they come primarily from Mexico or Central America or even Asia.

By and large, the old vision statement is now a memory for most congregations, and that memory is no longer sustainable. Classical music, lutefisk suppers, and sixteenth-century German liturgy are staples in this memory. One Lutheran leader says that most Lutheran congregations are looking forward with eager anticipation to either 1959 or 1968. If those years ever appear again, the church will be ready. Joy was, at this point, looking forward to 1959.

We also had the added drawback of having some volunteer leaders who had come as disgruntled members of other congregations. I have heard much advice that asserts that it is never wise to build a new congregation with the dissatisfied people from another. These people often will replicate their negative spirits in the new congregation. Unfortunately, this was already in place when I arrived. Persons who had been in the center of conflict where they formerly belonged now imposed the same attitudes upon us. Positive, visionary, loving people were in short supply at Joy.

The more I analyzed the community in which we were located, the more I realized that most of the people were not Lutheran and had never been Lutheran. Indeed, most of them were not Christian. Christ and the practices of the church were not a memory for a growing percentage of people in our community. The unchurched outnumbered the churched.

We needed a missionary spirit, a zeal for others at the very heart of our vision. Kennon Callahan, in *Effective Church Leadership,* asserts that missionary pastors are required for the future. "The day of the professional minister is over," he writes. "The day of the missionary pastor has come." The professional minister movement, which began in the late 1940s, ended quietly in the late 1980s with administrative gridlock. Professional ministers perform rather well in stable and declining churches, but not well in growing churches. "The day of the professional minister is over, *the day of the missionary pastor has come*" (Callahan, 3, emphasis added).

I assert, even further, that *the day of the missionary congregation has come.* Imagineering leadership means using all of the theological imagination God gives to us and then finding a way to engineer the specifics. We need both a vision and a strategy by which to carry it out. My first year at Joy had concentrated more on perish than on parish. We had no choice but to become a missionary church.

Our vision required us to reach out beyond our own membership. If all we had done was sit and wait for recently replanted Lutherans to show up, we might have waited forever. We did not have forever. Even if people had shown up at Joy, they would not have stayed for long when they caught a glimpse of the dysfunctional nature of our church.

All of You Who Belong to Nobody

Church leaders know far too well that most congregations spend most of their time talking to themselves and passing judgment on others. What we need to do is to spend our time talking to others and judging what we ourselves are doing.

 KEY DISCOVERY: Breakthrough mission begins with a compelling vision for mission.

Early in the second year of my ministry at Joy, we brought together a group of people for a weekend in order to look at our future. For the most part, these were people who believed we should reach out beyond our own membership. They were open to God's new vision. At that time we took our first steps into our future.

A vision statement that came from this retreat still is our guiding vision fifteen years later: *"That all may know Jesus Christ, and become a responsible member of his church, we share his love with joy inspired by the Holy Spirit."*

What a breakthrough! We now had a vision. The language and meaning of this short statement were revolutionary. Our clearly defined vision was no longer just to reach Lutherans. We were not here just for Norwegians, Swedes, or Germans. We were not even called only to minister to Christians. We wanted everyone to know Jesus Christ. Matthew 28:19-20a, the Great Commission, was the Scripture guiding our thinking: "Go therefore and make disciples of all nations, baptizing them in the name of the Father and of the Son and of the Holy Spirit, and teaching them to obey everything that I have commanded you." This was our all-encompassing vision. We wanted to be a church seeking to reach to all with the gospel, the good news of salvation in Jesus Christ. Of course we had heard this before. But we had to name and own it as *our* vision.

There was more, however. We wanted (and still want) people not only to know Jesus Christ but also to become a part of the people of God, the community of faith. In order to bring our vision to the world, we needed responsible partners who would bring the gifts, the faith, the discipline, the passion to carry out God's call. This meant participation in worship, education, mission, giving, and witness. Out of our experience with Jesus Christ and his church came the motivation to share God's abiding grace and love with others.

The Great Commission was only a part of the vision, for the Great Commandment was also essential. "You shall love the Lord your God with all your heart, and with all your soul, and with all your mind. . . . And . . . your neighbor as yourself" (Matt. 22:37, 39). We believed that the world would know we were Christians by our love. We envisioned becoming such a loving community that this love would overflow. Even those who were not a part of our community of faith would see that love, hear about it, and experience it. Love is centered in joy.

We wanted to love with joy. We wanted to create a sense of joy that would be contagious. We wanted to live up to our name. "Joy to the world, the Lord is come," we sang at Christmas. Our vision was to be a community of joy all year long. What greater vision could there be?

We affirmed that all our vision and action was empowered by the Holy Spirit. We were influenced by Martin Luther's interpretation of the third article of the Apostles' Creed: "I believe that I cannot by my own reason or strength believe in Jesus Christ or come to him, but that the Holy Spirit has called me through the Gospel, enlightened me with gifts, and sanctified and preserved me in the one true faith."

Our vision was God's doing. The Spirit of God supplied the power, a power greater than all our frustrations and limitations. We could never have done this on our own. Amazingly, we had been given the promise that we would do what Jesus had done and even greater things as well. Because of the gift of the Spirit, all things were possible.

I am inspired by the story of William Booth, the founder of the Salvation Army. Booth spent most of his years reaching out to the poor and needy on the streets of London. The following story may be apocryphal, but it has an important message.

Each Christmas there was a tradition in London that the churches would send out representatives to the streets to invite the poor to a Christmas celebration. Huge crowds would gather for this annual burst of generosity. The Anglicans would begin by announcing, "All of you who are Anglicans, come with us." Then it was the Roman Catholics: "All who are Catholic, come with us." Then the Methodists, the Lutherans, and all the other denominations announced, "Whoever belongs to us, come with us." Finally, when all of the church representatives had made their invitations, a large crowd of people still was milling about. At that point William Booth would shout out to the people, "All of you who belong to no one, come with me."

In a sense, this concern for the nobodies became our vision: "All of you people in northwest Phoenix who belong to no one, come with us. All who have not heard the gospel or have rejected it at some point in your lives, come with us. All who are weary and heavy laden, come with us, and God will give you rest. All who are in any kind of need, who are without hope, come with us. All who wish to be a part of a community where Christ is Lord and everybody is somebody, come with us. All who wish to be a part of a passionate vision and not just a church, come with us."

 KEY DISCOVERY: Vision produces powerful results.

In retrospect, I can see how truly incredible and presumptuous this vision was. We had a most inadequate facility, a site filled with weeds and debris, a congregation split between focusing on the past and focusing on the future. We had no staff, no money, no enthusiasm, and almost no people after my first year of ministry.

Yet God gave us a vision. We discovered that there was unbelievable power in such a vision. We now had a vision that could capture the imagination of our tiny flock. We had a vision that could touch the lives of those who had never been here before.

Our eyes were now on the vision, not on the problems. We were energized by what God was calling us to be. With a vision we could develop very clear strategies of where we wanted to go, and we could move intentionally in that direction.

Decision Time

Not all the remaining members of our congregation were enthralled with our new vision. We learned what most churches experience: When you craft a new vision, there will always be some who will decide that this is not their vision. They will find it the right time to move on. This is one of the most helpful parts of a vision: It gives people a decisive opportunity to sign on or sign off.

We also discovered, however, that most people are captured by a new vision. The more forward-looking and dynamic that vision is, the more people will want to become a part of making it happen. Without a vision, the people perish; but with a vision, a congregation can be poised for the future. Community Church of Joy would never be the same again.

 KEY DISCOVERY: A strategic plan + vision = powerful results.

An essential part of a vision is developing key strategies. Harley Swiggum, author of the Bethel Bible Series, once said that the difference between success and failure is the difference between a general and a specific objective. In the process of developing a vision, the easy way out is to focus only on the idea, the dream, the goal.

Without a specific plan, however, the dream will languish. Vision without action is just a dream. We needed to move very quickly to the next step of enfleshing the vision. What would it look like? What steps were needed to get there?

One denominational official warned me in no uncertain terms that becoming specific is the worst decision a church can make. If you set specific objectives, and then you do not reach them, you generate a climate of failure. We preferred the opposite approach: If you have specific goals, and you reach them or transcend them, you create a climate of success.

Even if we did not meet all the goals we had set, the process of working toward them would be invaluable. We would create a direction, a specific motivational goal, which would pull our church toward the future. However, if we had no idea where we were going or when we wanted to arrive, then any road would have sufficed.

Our strategies were not the vision. Our vision was to reach people for Jesus Christ and to help them become responsible disciples as members of our church. Under the leadership of the Holy Spirit, we wanted persons to share Christ's love with joy.

Our goals were ways of accomplishing the vision. Our vision was not to glorify buildings or to pave parking lots. We did not have a vision to create alternatives for worship or to build a staff. These were all merely steps that helped us carry out the vision.

Statistics, dollars, or programs were not the vision; they only helped the vision emerge with more clarity. At the initial leadership retreat, with a congregation of less than one hundred, we decided that we would grow to a church of three thousand members within ten years. Our vision was not to grow to include three thousand warm but passive bodies. Our vision was to reach people for Jesus Christ. We set specific numbers that would motivate us to carry out the vision. This gave us a way to measure how effective we were and to make other decisions that would tell us if our vision was still in focus.

Looking at the situation in a different way, we believed that if we were truly responding to God's vision for us, we would most likely become even a larger church. Three thousand people gathered together out of an urban population of two million is actually not a very substantial percentage.

We also projected that we would have a budget of one million dollars within ten years. Again, this budget was not our vision. We decided that we needed to raise that kind of money in order to be faithful to the vision of reaching people with the gospel. Again, the stark reality of the situation was overwhelming. When we set the new vision, we had a budget of $50,000 a year, and we were shrinking fast.

During the first meeting at which we presented our new vision, a very sincere elderly man stood up and responded, "Wait just a minute! All of this which we have heard is most impractical. We should not take this young pastor seriously, for he is only thirty years old. When he grows up, he will get a little more practical sense."

I was feeling like I had just been pulled through a clump of Arizona cacti. But those leaders who had been a part of creating the vision stood to defend the vision and to support me as the pastor. The vision now had a power of its own. People may have resisted various programs or personalities, but the vision had an integrity all its own. We were vision-driven, not personality- or program-led.

When we analyzed other congregations of three thousand members, we put together a staffing plan for the next decade. Once again, adding staff was not our vision. Our vision was reaching people for Jesus Christ. Building a staff was a strategy for carrying out the vision.

We realized that in a time when everyone was "church-connected" a church could rely on large numbers of volunteers to carry out most of the ministry. Today, the women, who in the past have done most of the volunteering, have entered the career world in overwhelming numbers. Thus in today's unchurched world, staffing becomes a crucial aspect of ministry. One outstanding staff member can vitalize an entire area of ministry. One marginal staff member can tear down a ministry.

We developed a ten-year plan for staffing, which demanded that we set priorities. What a gift this turned out to be! Over the past seventeen years, whenever we have needed to add new staff people, we have not had to deal with much resistance. The decision has already been made—in 1979. It is in the plan. We did not plan to fail.

We also separated the decision about new staff and programs from that of money. As I mentioned earlier, I have never let my decisions be based solely on financial considerations. Vision produces finances, not the other way around. During the ten years following the inception of our vision, we hired scores of staff members. Not one of them was ever hired with the money in hand. We have started virtually every new ministry without money but with plans for creative financing.

Usually, we have brought new staff into our ministry as volunteers. We find these people mostly within the congregation. Gradually we move them to part-time pay. Some eventually became full-time, although many will always be part-time. Lyle Schaller told us during a consultation that most churches today are staffed to decline—to fail. We want to be staffed for growth. The available money never should determine vision.

Creating a new vision was the turning point in the life and ministry of Joy. Our attempts to create a vision brought us face-to-face with God's vision for our congregation. We were transformed. Without a vision, there is no question that we would have perished; but a vision gave us new life and hope. Vision moved us from problems to possibilities. Vision helped us dream great dreams. Thank God for a vision!

▼ LIST YOUR KEY DISCOVERIES ▼

Most church leaders have been through a visioning process. But most of those visions are filed in a drawer and seldom enfleshed with planning. From the key discoveries in this chapter, reflect on times when visioning has become incarnate in your congregation. If you have internalized your congregation's vision, write it down here and describe specific instances where the vision drove the plan. If you think that your vision is but a memory, list three or more things that you can do to receive a new vision from God.

_____

_____

_____

_____

CHAPTER 3 COMPELLING WORSHIP

The aspect of church life most challenged by the forces of change is that of worship. Worship is also the stronghold for those who make their stand against change. That should not be surprising, for worship is the center of our life together as a Christian community. No event, no celebration, no coming together by believers has more impact and power than does worship.

In fact, in any congregation, if prayer, praise, and response do not happen in worship, they do not happen anywhere. If inspiration and hope and gospel-centered proclamation do not happen in worship, they often are in short supply. What takes place in other forums during the week can be life-affirming and at times even transforming, but if the worship life conveys apathy or is lifeless, then whatever else is bright seems to lose its luster. Worship is the heartbeat of the Christian church.

 KEY DISCOVERY: Worship is the workshop for transformational mission.

> *[God] put a new song in my mouth.*
> —Psalm 40:3

When I was a child growing up in rural Minnesota and South Dakota, it was no shocking revelation to me that our forms of worship were primarily for another generation. My peers and I were not the first to label much of what passed for worship as boring and irrelevant. We certainly were not the first to see the liturgical format, rich as it was, as increasingly passé.

We interpreted the Eurocentric ritual, the strange and ancient Elizabethan language, and the peculiar vestments as memories from a museum culture. Classical music simply did not communicate to us. When a pastor is chanting archaic language, it makes no connections with any part of contemporary life. It is hardly surprising that approximately 90 percent of my peers would leave after confirmation and not be seen in church again.

Some well-spoken theologians would like to "require" seekers and confirmands to learn this archaic "period" language in order to qualify as disciples of Jesus Christ. But confirmation has become something like teaching seekers an ancient language in four weeks and then expecting them to speak like Elizabethans for the rest of their lives. The graduates of such a course would rather pass through the strange elective course and move away, their baptism notwithstanding.

Coloring Outside the Lines

While leading gospel teams at Concordia College, I had the opportunity to create many new worship forms. The team I led spent the year experimenting with innovative combinations of music, drama, liturgy, and preaching. We had a distinct advantage: After the worship service was over, we could quickly leave town.

The gospel team movement at Concordia had wide participation and support. Outreach teams of students were organized to go out and perform at congregational and community events. I saw this as the vehicle by which I could pursue an interest in developing new music and worship resources.

Even though the implicit vision of Concordia for the outreach teams was to represent traditional Christian practices and music forms, there were a few innovators who saw that the world and the church were indeed changing. We had the freedom to utilize new forms. We played at church services, community celebrations, dances—whatever came along.

Coloring outside the lines became our purpose. Yet the college continued to showcase us at prime-time events. Soon we had more invitations than we could possibly accept. During my first three years of college, I found the competition for time and energy between our music ministry and academics to be consistently on the increase. We sensed it was time to try something new.

Mary and I made two life-changing decisions. The first was to be married at the end of our junior year. The second was to take a leave from school for a year and travel with an outreach team. We had no idea if there would be enough open doors to keep us busy for a year, but we decided to risk and trust.

Two church leaders believed in us and provided ongoing support: Dr. Art Grimstad from Concordia and Dr. Conrad Thompson, director of evangelism for the American Lutheran Church. With such support, we had confidence to launch out. We named our group "Earthrise Singers," packed our suitcases and instruments, and went on the road.

In one place after another we found people who enthusiastically responded to new forms of Christian worship and music. In fact, people were hungry for something that scratched where they itched. Spending most of our time in village churches, we found heartwarming support and enthusiasm.

I had a growing conviction that we were on the right track. Clearly God was leading us into some new and uncharted waters. We had our most dramatic support from the disaffected and the indifferent. Those who were on the fringe of the power often demonstrated the most enthusiasm.

Resistance to our style of worship and music was also not hard to uncover. In *The Once and Future Church*, Loren Mead suggests that there are three expected responses to the shift from Christendom to post-Christendom. The first is denial. We tend to deny that which we find the most painful to accept. Many church leaders and theologians will not admit that the world is changing—that the old forms and practices are no longer suited to reach contemporary culture. Denial is very real.

The second is the attempt to return to Christendom. Mead says that this is a popular response of the religious right. We find it in the middle of the mainline as well: "Let's go back to being a Christian nation"; "Let's be Lutherans [or Catholics or Methodists and so on] and eliminate all intrusions of secularity"; "Get rid of that dangerous subversive music!"

The third response is to accept the change and then to find a proactive response. We see some glimmers of hope but not too many. Resistance to change is stronger than any acceptance of the revolution that is obvious around us.

When we began to present a new kind of music and worship in our travels, there were some who asserted that we were tearing down standards and practices rather than building up legitimate forms of Christian praise. We tried to communicate that while Jesus Christ is the same yesterday, today, and forever, the way we worship and sing to God cannot always be the same. Resistance to change of this kind is the most fierce and warlike of all.

Yet many exciting stories of change also accompanied our travels. At one concert an obviously troubled young woman stood up in front, attentive to our music. In conversation with her during one of the breaks, we heard her story about alcoholic parents. Her heart was broken. She came to the concert with thoughts of suicide, but the music and message deeply touched her life, and she was open to Christ's love and hope. Later communication informed us that her life had indeed changed direction that evening, and she was learning new, positive, fruitful ways of living.

Money was constantly an issue as we traveled. Freewill offerings were often not very lucrative. But I have never allowed money or the lack of it to determine my plans. Perhaps growing up with nothing as the son of an itinerant pastor gave me freedom from worry. The worst that could happen is that I would have nothing again.

 KEY DISCOVERY: On faith, commit a year to an itinerant evangelism ministry.

Upon returning to Concordia for our senior year, Mary and I had the conviction that God had something truly exciting and even revolutionary ahead of us. The year of travel had been an incredible time of learning and experimentation. I recommend this kind of risk taking—committing a year on faith to an itinerant evangelism ministry—to all budding seminarians. It makes you ready for something new, and your faith during times of change will inspire great confidence. After that year we yearned for a new risk, but we had no clue as to what it would be.

The Praise of God Will Always Change

Up to this point, I had not wavered one inch in my decision never to become a pastor. I never wanted to find myself in a situation where a congregation could abuse and humiliate me as my father's congregation had done to him. Furthermore, our year on the road had brought us into contact with numerous pastors who were discouraged and defeated, who wished they had been doing anything else. So I wanted to stay away from any kind of congregational church leadership.

I was convinced that God had called me to be on the edge. I was to use my music and my ability to organize others into teams in a ministry to serve Jesus Christ. I began to dream that I could be a part of a new movement in the church.

Above all, we attempted to translate the language of the Scriptures into today's metaphors and stories, to use words and narrative forms that would speak to people born in the latter part of the twentieth century. As European church composers had done in the past, we chose music that was similar to the kinds of music people listened to all week long—but with Christian words and symbols. The gospel does not change, but the way we proclaim it must always change. God does not change, but the way we worship and praise God will always change, like it or not.

We were truly following in the steps of Martin Luther, who translated the gospel into the language of the common people. We too were constantly trying to find new ways to translate the gospel and the message of Jesus and his saving love into language and forms that people today could understand. In our creative attempts at new forms of worship, our target audience was not lifelong Christians, not those steeped in Christian tradition, many of whom are bound by ethnic or tribal loyalties. We were proactively responding to those who were on the edge or were not even yet on the edge.

I have had the basic conviction for much of my ministry that there are plenty of congregations to reach those wanting to keep tradition alive. Those churches that are earnestly trying to reach out to the unchurched, the seekers, the marginalized, and the drifting are urgently needed. It became our vision to discover new ways to present the gospel and then to encourage other congregations to innovate as well.

Whenever I helped implement new worship forms, the response was nothing short of remarkable. New visions for worship did indeed capture the imagination and the spirit of persons, especially those who had been on the outside of the church. By re-creating the ways we did worship, we were bringing together entirely new communities of faith—and we were launching new traditions and practices.

Our ideas of worship have always marked a radical departure from business as usual. In the early 1970s, we were most assuredly challenging the tones of the times. Our work was in turn resisted by the forces of the status quo. Many told us that we were moving down a slippery slope. We were watering down the tradition. Some even accused us of selling out Jesus to the gods of success.

Our sense as we traveled with the gospel team was that one period of history was ending, and another was beginning. If the Christian church could not understand the changing paradigm, it might die along with the old. The number of congregations we found who were experimenting with alternative worship was minuscule. The time for any acceptance of innovation had still not arrived.

We learned that alternative forms of worship must be a priority for a congregation if worship is to be effective. A specific time should be set aside for this form of worship, and the time must be observed consistently. Constant shifting of hours and styles of worship confuses the congregation. It is always better that the worshiping congregation not be surprised, but know what to expect and when to expect it.

We also learned that alternative worship is better scheduled at the later hours on Sunday morning. This is the time when the young people and those who are on the fringe are much more likely to attend. Above all we learned that the key to alternative worship is musical leadership of the highest possible quality.

 KEY DISCOVERY: Learn how to create inspiring, inviting worship.

Fresh in my mind as I arrived at Joy in the late 1970s was a presentation David Preus, then the president of the American Lutheran Church, made at a gathering of American Lutheran ministers. He strongly asserted:

> After thirty-nine years of being a pastor, I have to say that our greatest public sin is that we are boring. Lack of an evangelizing tradition has hurt growth, but dull worship services may be the most devastating problem of all. Our sermons are not so much heretical as they are uninteresting. We distrust excitement, and we are not even sure about enthusiasm. . . . A visitor at our worship services is likely to figure out that the most exciting part is trying to understand where you are between bulletin and hymnal, standing and sitting, and passing the collection plate.

I also recall with much agreement the words of Ray Bakke, a profound thinker about ministry to the city. In his book *The Urban Christian*, he suggests that Martin Luther advised each great church council to study the issues of faith and life in its generation.

> Some groups all through history have had complete sets of concrete, cultural practices which they regard as almost synonymous with the Gospel. Their witness to Christ is frozen into cultural forms which are irrelevant or unintelligible to most people. They become museum churches with period lifestyles, music, dress, and vocabulary. Evangelism for these believers carries all of this cultural baggage. The way to the cross is through the door of their traditions. (Bakke, 57)

Our congregation, Joy, was at the time of my arrival indeed frozen into forms of the past, and we had much company among mainline churches. What we were doing might have made sense in 1959, and perhaps it still did to those who were born and raised in the Lutheran, ethnic village churches; but it was completely out of reach for the utter secularity of late-twentieth-century Phoenix.

When our vision was born to reach out to all people with the gospel of Jesus Christ, there was no question that worship was one of the first places we needed to examine. Once our evangelistic vision was in place, we had no choice but to change our worship.

How Pre-Christians Think

George Hunter, from Asbury Theological Seminary, spoke at our annual worship-evangelism conference, and he highlights our experience in his book *How to Reach Secular People* (Nashville: Abingdon, 1992). Many of his insights helped us understand the kind of people we were trying to reach. I will try to briefly summarize some of his main points.

1. *"Secular people are essentially ignorant of basic Christianity."* Most are biblically illiterate, and many are misinformed about essential Christianity. As Alan Walker of Australia observes, Christian knowledge and awareness are now the echo of an echo, or even an echo too faint to be audible.

Such people feel awkward or embarrassed upon entering a sacred building, and may never even think about being a part of a congregation. They are almost completely ignorant of the Christian stories and biblical allusions offered from most traditional pulpits.

2. *"Secular people are seeking life* before *death."* Most contemporary secular people are life-oriented. Much of history has been dominated by tragedy—famines, epidemics, plagues. People were obsessed with death and longed for life after death. Today most people are frightened more by the prospect of nonexistence than by the threat of everlasting torment. They wish for abundant life in the present more than they anticipate a heavenly reward.

3. *"Secular people are conscious of doubt more than guilt."* Doubt presents the most important feature of the secular audience. In Christendom, people were motivated more by

guilt, and even non-Christians felt responsible for seeking forgiveness and absolution from guilt.

Today many people attribute society's problems to guilt, but to someone else's guilt. Most people who feel personal guilt seek help from therapists and self-help books rather than from pastors and sacred writings. Doubt has replaced guilt as the primary characteristic of the secular person.

4. *"Secular people have a negative image of the Church."* They have no confidence in the church as an intelligent, relevant, or credible institution. Fallen televangelists exacerbate the problem. Today, people trust science and common sense more than religion because they recall how often the church has been proven wrong.

People began to question the church when it began reacting defensively to the the findings of modern science, the diversity of cultures and beliefs, and other events of "secularization." In addition, many people have made generalizations about all churches based on their experiences with particular churches that seemed lifeless or out of touch. Most people are not angry at the church, just indifferent.

5. *"Secular people have multiple alienations."* In Christendom, it seems, people met their needs for belonging through their work, through the community or village in which they lived, and through their extended families. Today, however, people are often alienated from nature, from neighbors, from political and economic systems, from their work. Hunter quotes Bruce Larson, who asserts that alienated people are characteristically lonely and that some medical professionals claim that loneliness is the number-one killer in America.

Hunter concludes that most secular people find Christianity to be boring. Those raised in an entertainment age on television sitcoms find church to be insufficiently interesting or stimulating. Secular people almost inevitably find a cultural barrier, or what he calls the "stained glass" barrier. When they do enter a church, they find the experience to be culturally alienating.

KEY DISCOVERY: Learn to know how
pre-Christian secular people think.

If secular people do not understand the jargon, relate to the music, know when to stand up or sit down, identify with the people, or feel comfortable in the facility, they infer that Christianity and the Christian God are not for people like them. *This cultural barrier is usually not perceived by the church,* especially when the target population bears many of the same characteristics (age-group, socioeconomic status, educational background, recreational interests, and so on) as the church members. We simply assume that they do understand and relate to what we feel comfortable doing.

Secular people are not "churchbroken"; church is usually a different subculture for them. This cultural barrier is sometimes crossed when earnest seekers agree to be baptized. They submit to reinculturation and become like church people. That happens often enough to seduce church people into thinking there is no cultural barrier or that all seekers should be eager to adopt our ways.

But churches that would reach much greater numbers of secular people *must pay the price of identifying more strongly with the people in their mission field.* They must remove the cultural barrier that presently keeps most people from considering the faith itself.

 KEY DISCOVERY: Cross over the river of
change at the narrowest point.

Eighty-seven people attended our one worship service the first year I was at Joy. While this may seem like a negative experience, remember that at least one-half of all congregations in North America average no more than eighty-seven in attendance on a Sunday. Surrounded as we were with so many thousands of unchurched people, however, I was appalled at this tepid response.

Most of our worshipers were lifelong church members. They expressed little or no interest in reaching anyone other than people just like us. The pressure to keep the status quo is incessant. Sometimes I think that the English translation for *status quo* should be "mess." We were in the midst of the status quo, and we indeed had a mess.

As we began to create a new vision, a wildly optimistic goal of growing to three thousand members within a decade also emerged. One of the ways we believed that we could accomplish the vision was to change our worship. We were determined to offer alternatives, not to abandon that which many held dear. We wanted to cross over the river of change at the narrowest point.

Even that decision provoked controversy. When we proposed that we move from one worship service to two and that the later service be an alternative format, shock waves reverberated throughout the congregation. It was clear that many did not share the vision and that they did not care about reaching the unchurched. All they wanted to do was protect the status quo. As they had regarding the issue of expanding the staff, the leaders who created the new vision prevailed. Plans were made to add a service.

One year after I arrived at Joy, we moved to a two-service format. The 9:00 A.M. worship was our traditional worship service; our 11:00 A.M. service was the alternative. The results were instructive. We managed to hold on to almost all the eighty-seven worshipers at the early service, but we added fifty to the later service.

Of those fifty choosing the alternative, about one-half were nonmembers. They were attracted by the new style of worship. Thus our overall attendance increased by close to 50 percent when we went from one service to two, which is not an uncommon experience. If a congregation wishes to increase worship attendance, one of the best ways is to increase the number of services. The other way is to add some form of alternative worship.

What happened at Joy over the next five years was that the later service continued to expand. Eventually we added a third worship service during the middle of the morning at 10:00. That quickly became our largest service, for 10:00 is truly prime time for worship. Attendance at 11:15 was next in numbers, and the lowest attendance was at 8:45.

In fact, after five years the early service still had approximately eighty-seven people. Many of the faces had changed, but the numbers were consistent. Almost all the growth had taken place in the two alternative worship services.

Seventeen years after the vision was received, we have five different styles of worship each weekend. Four services, each with its own style, are on Sunday, and one is on Saturday evening. I am not suggesting that anyone else can adopt this schedule, but it works for us because of our particular setting, space, history, and vision. Here is a brief description of each of our five services.

Saturday Evening, 6:00: Contemporary Country

Phoenix in many ways is in the heart of country-western culture. This worship service reflects that climate. The usually brief service is led by Tim Wright and the Good News Band.

Order of Service

Call to Worship	Good News Band
Welcome	
Opening Song	
Special Feature	
Gifts	Good News Band
Message	
Closing	

Sunday Morning, 8:30: Spirited Traditional

The service is led by the choir, focusing on singing hymns and songs. Substantial participation of the congregation is encouraged and obtained. We use selected parts of the traditional liturgy, and this service has the ambience of a mainline church service. It tends to attract many of our members who have been lifelong Christians. Here is a chance to enjoy our heritage and sing favorite hymns.

Sunday Morning, 9:30: Contemporary Blend

This service is led by the choir, blending both familiar songs and new alternatives. It has less congregational participation and more presentation. The worshipers are primarily members of the church, plus longtime visitors. It attracts those who enjoy some tradition, albeit a different tradition from what many of them experienced in the past. Variety and tradition are coordinated.

Sunday Morning, 10:30: New Contemporary

The music shifts quite dramatically at this service. Even less congregational singing and more presentation, such as drama and personal interviews, are common. More of the leading is done by the musical team. We are now focusing on the unchurched, visitors, and younger people. We appeal to those who want a new style of worship. We do not ask for as much participation because these people have had much less church experience. They are often hesitant or embarrassed at putting too much of themselves into the service.

Sunday Morning, 11:30: Modern Contemporary

The music here bears almost no resemblance to anything traditional. This music is very upbeat, contemporary, and designed to reach secular people. We focus strongly on baby boomers, ages thirty to fifty, and baby busters, ages twenty to thirty. This service is populated by those people who do not know our songs, our creeds, or our traditions.

Most have never even sung a hymn or attended a church supper. They are nervous about even being in a church. They fear that the culture will be alien to them. The volume of the music rises all morning long. At this service we almost blow the roof off the sanctuary. Yet while the music changes, the words center on Jesus Christ, on the Cross, on the Resurrection, on new life. Music is meant to accomplish the vision, reaching unchurched people.

▼ LIST YOUR KEY DISCOVERIES ▼

Worship planning always involves being open to change. If the vision is to reach people with the gospel of Jesus Christ, then the strategy is to provide the kind of worship alternatives that will accomplish the vision. There is practically no way to create a set of standardized worship practices that will be effective in every setting. The congregation needs to begin with God and God's vision, then implement the means that will enable them to see the vision become reality. Different forms of worship are not the vision, they are meant to carry out the vision.

Reflect on the kinds of worship that you experience now in your congregation. Give a name to those styles and write them down. Now think of one or two populations of unchurched people in your region that you have been called to reach. Write down the kind of music that each population prefers, and see if your vision can be carried out through these alternatives.

_____

_____

_____

_____

CHAPTER 4 TAKING THE CHURCH PUBLIC

Worship the LORD with gladness.
—Psalm 100:2

 KEY DISCOVERY: It is important to take the local congregation public.

Is worship necessarily public? So much worship today in Christian churches is private. Strangers have no idea what is taking place. Worship is only for members of the family. And sometimes that family includes only the individual in private prayer before God. Our vision immediately made us a public institution. We believe that all should know Jesus Christ. If worship is the center of our life together, then it must be public.

In order to become more effective at reaching out to people beyond our own membership at Community Church of Joy, we have changed not only our music but also our preaching. We believe strongly in the spoken proclamation of the gospel, in the clear and unequivocal message of God's saving love, but we realize that in this entertainment age of technology and music videos, preaching must also change.

Some years ago we established a *Message Research and Evaluation Team.* We invite worshipers, both members and nonmembers, to help us communicate as effectively as possible. We ask this group to help us prepare messages that speak to the real needs of people and also to evaluate how well we are doing. We invite people for this task who have particular gifts in the areas of creativity, research, writing, biblical knowledge, and fact gathering.

Such a process takes substantial advanced planning. Scripture passages and themes are chosen many months in advance by those doing the preaching. This information is then given to the Message Research and Evaluation Team to help them in their planning. The participants focus their attention on providing insights, illustrations, and feedback for the message preparation.

We encourage those on the teams to hold two different viewpoints in tension. On the one hand, we want them to very consciously hold to their own Christian beliefs and values as they study and respond. On the other hand, we want them to develop a secular perspective so that they can better target the larger public we are trying to reach.

We have prepared a rather extensive manual that we give to all members of the Message Research and Evaluation Team. In that manual we have developed a list of basic guidelines that help them in their work. Some of these are as follows:

1. Submit excerpts from books, magazines, newspapers, poems, songs, Bible commentaries, and other sources that provide background and interesting material to relate or build on. These can be centered in the past, present, or future.

2. Submit a list of concise points related to the topic. These may be conclusions, trends, suggestions, analogies, predictions, problems, solutions, surprises, historical vignettes, spiritual absolutes.

3. Look for statistics that relate to the topic and objectives. (Magazine articles often provide the most current statistics.)

4. Try to submit at least one humorous story or interesting real-life illustration that relates to the theme and the objectives.

5. Look for illuminating quotations or phrases (or create your own) that are catchy "hooks" to hold people's attention and help focus the message. Be a wordsmith.

6. You may wish to include a real-life story out of your personal experience or some reflection of your own.

7. Watch for visual enhancements such as video clips, slides, and other visually engaging materials.

As might be expected, our preaching has changed dramatically as we have become more and more attuned to the public audience we seek to reach. During my first years as a preacher, I sought to preach sermons that were models of theological consistency, quoting many of the foremost theologians. I found myself still trying to speak to my seminary professors and classmates. The problem was that they weren't the ones listening to me. I was truly appealing to lifelong Christians. I soon learned that unchurched people did not have the foggiest notion of what I was talking about. I needed a new vocabulary and method if I was to communicate with secular people.

I decided to put away my manuscript and retire the pulpit. Words and images were simplified. I geared our messages to those who had not been here before rather than to the longtime members. I decided not to try to cover everything all at once, but to touch on the areas of life that were of most concern to the unchurched. I wanted my preaching to bring about a sense of trust and openness so that I could encourage people to begin a spiritual journey.

I also learned the essential importance of affirmation and encouragement. Studies indicate that up to 80 percent of the messages many people receive each day are negative. One man told me, "I get beat up all week long. I don't come to church to have you do the same." An appropriate use of the law is important, but we want to center on the gospel. Jesus Christ is good news.

In recent years I also have become aware of the importance of different voices in the preaching ministry. At one time I thought that I could communicate best with all the people. Now I have learned that different preachers reach different audiences. Thus at the present time Pastor Paul Sorenson preaches at the 8:15 Sunday morning worship service. He is more effective than I am at communicating with those who are lifelong Christians. Pastor Tim Wright preaches at the 11:30 Sunday morning and the 6:00 Saturday evening services. He has learned how to communicate with the most secular people who visit Joy.

I preach at the 9:30 and 10:30 Sunday morning worship services, where the worshiping congregations are more in the middle in terms of theology and worship style. I am not sure that I am quite prepared to be relegated to the middle, but when I breezed past my fortieth birthday some years back and when our son Patrick celebrated birthday number twenty-four recently, I sensed I was entering the middle stage of my life.

 KEY DISCOVERY: Keep on inviting community leaders to worship with you.

In all our worship planning, we have been attempting to move from private to public. I am reminded of a story Robert Schuller tells of an event that took place earlier in his ministry. He was returning from out of town and was taking a taxi to his home. As the taxi passed by the Garden Grove Community Church (now the Crystal Cathedral), Schuller and the driver could see the huge thirteen-story Christian life center with the lighted cross on the top.

Schuller asked the driver, "Sir, do you see that tall building? Can you tell me what that might be?" The taxi driver never hesitated: "That is a large insurance company."

Schuller concluded right then and there that his church was still too private.

One of the most creative ways we have discovered to go public is to honor people in our community who have demonstrated extraordinary compassion and unusual commitment to serving the needs of others. By featuring such people, we give the message to those who worship at Joy that this is God's call for each of us. We are called to live not for ourselves but for others.

For example, at the time of Desert Storm, as we were facing the unsettling confrontation with Iraq in the Persian Gulf, the Phoenix newspapers gave much publicity to the work of Cindy McCain. What was noteworthy was that Cindy McCain was leading the first medical team to Kuwait, responding directly to the many children who were being injured and killed by land mines planted by the retreating Iraqi soldiers.

Ms. McCain and her medical team went to Kuwait in order to bring healing and hope to badly scarred children. Out of our appreciation for these efforts, we invited Cindy to come to Joy on a Sunday morning so that we could honor her and give her a distinguished service award.

Public notice was taken of this event, partly because Cindy is the wife of Senator John McCain of Arizona, but also because of the visibility of her medical team in the media. A number of leaders from the state participated in honoring Cindy during our Sunday morning service. In addition to bestowing this honor, we gained a great deal of visibility among people who most likely knew little about us.

An added benefit, which we did not anticipate, is that the McCain family have continued to worship with us at Joy and have become strong supporters of our ministry. In fact, when Cindy McCain received the very prestigious Citizen of the World award in Washington, D.C., with Henry Kissinger as the featured speaker, I was asked to give the opening address.

We are constantly seeking to affirm and honor people who are making a difference on behalf of others. We want to highlight living examples of the Great Commandment. Every time we recognize others in this way, we ourselves move from private to public.

George Gallup's research tells us that close to one-half of all Americans claim some kind of profound religious experience that has changed their lives forever. Unfortunately, many of them are not encouraged in traditional churches to talk about these miraculous events in their lives, not even with the pastor. The result is that many of them have gone elsewhere.

The McCains reminded us as a congregation about how God's Spirit intervenes at some of the most surprising moments. When their son was born, the doctors noticed immediately that he had an erratic heartbeat. After rather frantically trying to bring the problem under control, the medical team finally gathered the McCain family together and told them it was no use. Their child was going to die.

Immediately the McCains asked if the hospital chaplain could come and baptize their baby. He did, and at the very moment when the chaplain put the water on the head of the tiny infant and baptized him in the name of the Father, Son, and Holy Spirit, the baby's heart began to beat regularly.

A miracle had taken place. Soon the baby was completely healthy. The doctors could only describe this as a miracle. The McCains told us most emphatically that they believe in miracles.

Our vision is to reach people with the gospel of Jesus Christ and then to help them become responsible members of his church. Attracting the secular audience to Joy and then finding ways to communicate effectively with them is only the beginning strategy. Our ultimate goal is to move them very quickly from consumerism to commitment, from being spectators to being servants.

We are the first to recognize that worship is not the place where dramatic change takes place in most people. Rather, it most often serves as a place of introduction, of invitation to commitment. We intentionally offer inspiration, hope, and encouragement in a climate of unconditional love and grace. We attempt to give those who attend something to take home with them, something practical, life-affirming, and sustaining.

Recently, one of the leaders of our congregation told me that the week past had been one of the most difficult of his entire life. Because of staff cutbacks in his company, he was forced to make an absolutely gut-wrenching decision. He had to fire his best friend. When he came to worship he was trying to nurse a broken heart. We offered him healing, hope, and comfort.

 KEY DISCOVERY: The Christian church needs to be even friendlier than Disneyland.

Pat Keifert, an innovative seminary professor, popularized the phrase, "Hospitality to the Stranger," or "Welcoming the Stranger." We have made a concerted effort to offer the best hospitality we are capable of providing.

We named this area of congregational life "Guest Relations," and we now even have a full-time staff person who is responsible for all aspects of this ministry. We believe that people ought to be treated with as much care and sensitivity when they come to church as they are when they visit a first-rate hotel or restaurant.

Thus we have developed a very intentional process of training greeters, hosts and hostesses, and ushers in hospitality and welcoming. We try to make our entire site as welcoming to strangers as possible, with quality signs and extra-clean and accessible bathrooms. We want to communicate to people that we are thrilled that they have come and we wish for them to return.

I learned again recently the utmost importance of hospitality. Before speaking at a conference in Syracuse, New York, I arrived early and was going to walk to the front of the arena to find a seat near the podium. Before I could enter an usher stood in my path and said rather authoritatively, "I cannot let you go in there."

I was rather taken aback by the confrontational attitude of this man, even a bit offended. I finally said to him, "I am the speaker for this event, and I need to sit somewhere near the front." Only then did he relent (somewhat reluctantly) and step aside so that I could make my way to the front of the auditorium.

I watched him meet the next group who entered the hall. Again he blocked them and would not let them enter. Someone asked the usher why they could not sit anywhere they pleased. His answer, "Then I would not have a job." His vision needed to be reinterpreted. His role should have been that of one who welcomed strangers, one who demonstrated hospitality.

 KEY DISCOVERY: Effective churches are invitational, not confrontational.

I walked into a Roman Catholic church recently for a meeting. To my surprise, just inside the front door a large Irish setter was vigorously wagging his tail, inviting me to stop and pet him. I could not get over how calming this welcoming, beautiful animal seemed to be.

When I eventually met with the priest I told him, with tongue in cheek, that I had just received one of the warmest welcomes I had ever received in a church, by an incredibly friendly dog. I expected the priest to be surprised. Perhaps even mortified. He simply replied, however, "I like to put my dog out in the front of the church. The children simply cannot wait to come and see him every week. He dispenses the most hospitality we have ever had." I knew this priest understood the importance of the welcome, unlike the usher I had encountered earlier.

The gospel of Jesus Christ is a word to be proclaimed in public, not just spoken or acted out in private. The church that follows Jesus as Lord and Savior also needs to be public. We are not called to flee from the world but rather to go into the world with the love and grace of God. The entire worship experience needs to connect with the public. Music and rituals and language have to communicate even with strangers.

Most Christian congregations today are private. Our challenge is that most are invisible, and even people on the same block and around the corner have no idea that the congregation exists. We determined early on that Joy would be public. "God so loved the world"—not just the church.

We have learned that the most effective evangelism happens when one person who is excited about the gospel, excited about our worship, invites another person. All studies show that most new people who show up at worship are invited by people they know. The more we touch the lives of people who worship at Joy, the more they become evangelists.

An essential key is worship. Our vision is that all might know Jesus Christ and become responsible members of his church. Our strategy has been to create five very different worship experiences and to make them as public as possible. Because people feel the presence of the Holy Spirit at our church, we are welcoming hundreds of new members each year. As we become more and more of a public church, we expect that growth to accelerate.

▼ LIST YOUR KEY DISCOVERIES ▼

Do you think that your congregation is more private than public? Write an answer first in terms of Sabbath worship and then in terms of the regional, community environment. How easy is it for a guest in the church to participate in worship prior to becoming a member?

_____

_____

_____

_____

5 PRAYER AND EVANGELISM

Prayer is meant to be the foundation of the church. Prayer is what gives us our life and power. Without prayer we are destined to expend more and more of our energy, with less and less impact. Eventually we burn out. Without prayer we will truly be on our own, relying only on our own resources. Without prayer we could not lead or minister for the long term.

Charles Allen, in a lecture at the Billy Graham School of Evangelism, told a story of a man who arrives at a train station in the dead of winter and notices that everyone in the station is barefoot. Thinking this absurd, he corners the first person he can find and asks the obvious question, "Why is everyone barefoot?"

The person looks rather dumbfounded at the question, then replies, "That's the question, isn't it? That is the question."

Walking outside into the snow and cold, the man is struck again by the sight of everyone barefoot. A second time he goes up to a passerby and asks the same question, "Tell me, sir, why is everyone barefoot? It's freezing out here." The reply is the same, "That is the question. That is the question."

Finally, almost desperately, the man asks still another person. "Why are your going barefoot? Have you never heard about shoes?"

"Oh," says the stranger, "just across the street we have a huge shoe factory. We are very proud of the shoe industry."

"Well, then, why are you not wearing any of these shoes?"

"That is the question," is the reply, "that is the question."

 KEY DISCOVERY: Prayer works!

The Lord accepts my prayer.
—Psalm 6:9

I have been given an absolutely incredible gift of prayer, which fits my Christian life like a pair of shoes. Prayer has changed the world, prayer has brought about amazing miracles, and prayer has given to each of us hope and comfort and power. Then why am I so often bare and naked without prayer to cover me? Why do we so seldom see prayer in the center of our church life, of our own lives?

That is the question, isn't it? That is the question. We have been given such a life-transforming gift, so why do we so often ignore it? That is the question.

Prayer is the foundation, the soul, of the Christian body. Whatever the particular circumstance of my life, I have always known that I can "take it to the Lord in prayer." Each morning I set aside my quiet time for prayer, which is what gives me the strength, the conviction, and the passion for the gospel the rest of the day. Even with all the motivational talk and the well-conceived strategies, without prayer, the vision will perish.

Sometimes, of course, prayer is all that a pastor can afford. When our vision was incubating, I often felt very much alone, without many allies or friends. I would cry out with repeated regularity to God and ask for help and strength just to endure. I often believed that I could not stand much more. I was near the breaking point, but the nourishment of God was always sufficient.

KEY DISCOVERY: Pruning the vision stimulates new growth.

Several years after coming to Joy, my life and ministry seemed to have lost their savor. I had reached a plateau, and I was feeling very frustrated. We had made numerous positive changes over the years, but we were now being challenged to move to a more demanding level of ministry and commitment. I was not sure that I had the faith or the leadership skills to do that.

When, on some days, I found myself in the midst of one storm after another, I would wish for a quiet harbor where I would be protected from the strident voices and keepers of yesterday's vision. I decided that I needed a new perspective. Thus I moved into a period of intensive graduate school education, hoping to earn a doctorate. Above all I hoped for renewal and a new understanding of what God was calling our church to be.

One afternoon while in school my feelings of uncertainty were especially strong. I decided to commit the rest of the day to prayer and fasting. I wanted to listen to God and see if I could discern where I was being called for the next period of my life. I could see that I was at a crossroads, and I needed a new focus.

The more I prayed, the more my mind and heart were filled with a long list of possibilities. Some of these ideas were brand new to me, going far beyond what I had ever before envisioned. Almost without warning, the daylight fled away and I was gazing out on the flashing lights of the city, which were contrasted against the darkness of the heavens above.

As I drank in the beauty of God's creation, as I stared out into the darkness that was dotted with the brilliant light, new life and creativity started flowing back into me. I took my notebook and began to write. I wrote as fast as my fingers would move. I had no idea of all that was inside me until I began to put it to paper. Writing is often the best way for me to listen to what God has placed upon my heart.

Before the evening was over, I had fleshed out some rather unbelievable blueprints for the next phase of my life and ministry. I had no idea of the source for many of these ideas. I certainly had never consciously considered them before, but there they were, on the paper. Now I had to deal with them, had to let them challenge me. If I had not written them down, I would have forgotten many of them.

When I shared these new insights with my professor, he interpreted them as a gift from God. He prayed with me and asked God to confirm this revelation to me.

Later, as I reflected on that evening of prayer, fasting, and journal writing, I was not at all sure how to interpret the results. I believed in miracles. I had witnessed so many instances of miracles in the lives of others. There was no other way to explain what had happened to them. Yet I had always hesitated to talk about anything supernatural in my own life. I had always been very careful to not put too much stock in any kind of mystical experience. At that particular moment, however, I was convinced that God had poured into me a new vision. I also sensed being filled with a new power and commitment that were beyond anything I had ever known.

 KEY DISCOVERY: Prayer is refreshment.

One of the specific visions that was confirmed that evening was the conviction that *prayer is to be the wellspring of Joy.* As our growth was accelerating, as we were building momentum, it was tempting for us to put most of our confidence in ourselves and in our own successes. While we had strongly believed in prayer in the past, for the most part it had tended to be just another program in the church.

Meanwhile, to keep us from thinking too highly of our efforts, we were vaguely aware of those who asserted that our approach to entertainment evangelism had created a candy-coated Christian experience, offering passive entertainment and a shopping-mall menu of anointed things for sale.

I now saw the vision very differently. *"That all may know Jesus Christ, and become a responsible member of his church, we share his love with joy inspired by the Holy Spirit."* Prayer would no longer be a program, a resource among other resources for this vision. Prayer needed to become the very source of our church, the fountain that would gush forth life in the desert. We believed that with prayer all things were possible. But prayer needed to be raised to a higher place. Prayer needed to become the most essential discipline that we would teach to those who worshiped in our congregation.

With this conviction in mind, we moved quickly to call a man named Björn Pedersen to become our minister of prayer. Björn had been working in another capacity on our staff, and we knew him to be a person with a unique gift of prayer. If this ministry was to be centered in prayer, then we needed someone to lead us in this emphasis.

We were highly cognizant that Joy was living on the edge, taking risks and climbing mountains. We could see that our risk taking would not only continue but accelerate. We had learned that whenever we attempted to change some basic paradigms of ministry, the level of resistance was high. We could only see more opposition in the future. Therefore, we were certain that we needed the power of God, the power that comes through prayer. Undergirding our efforts of ministry at every step of the way had to be the grace and love of God through Jesus Christ. Even though we were destined to be misunderstood and maligned, we knew God to be affirming and encouraging.

Since that time we have had a virtual explosion in the number of persons who seek God in prayer. *Dunamis*, the New Testament Greek word that means "power," has been released. At the present time we have two thousand people a month involved in some kind of prayer ministry, and there is no more fundamental practice for Christians to have.

KEY DISCOVERY: Every great church intentionally makes prayer a priority.

Prayer teams, prayer colleges, prayer groups, prayer seminars, prayer classes, prayer vigils, and prayer partnerships are all a part of this ministry. I am convinced that because all of us in leadership at Joy know that we have prayer partners who are praying for us every day and night, who are undergirding us all with prayer all the time, we have been given a power that is beyond any human dimension.

Some of us who have the gift of initiating new visions cannot spend most of our day in prayer, but we know that we are held up and blessed by those who have the gift and commitment to pray. We have set a goal to recruit up to two thousand personal intercessors by the year 2000, who are to join with other burgeoning prayer networks around the globe.

One event in the life of Joy highlighted the vitality and immediacy of prayer. I drove into the church parking lot one evening and found police cars everywhere. Two teenagers had gotten into an argument, and it had escalated into a life-and-death struggle. One of the boys had pulled out a knife and stabbed the other in the heart and the lung. Shortly after I arrived, a helicopter came to transport the critically wounded boy to the hospital. Most of the other teenagers gathered back into the church to pray.

I contacted our prayer partners and asked them to begin praying immediately for the healing of this boy. I rushed to the hospital and met the parents of the injured boy in the emergency room. We arrived in time to pray with the boy before he was taken into surgery.

After we waited for quite a long time, the surgeons reappeared to tell us that the only thing that had saved the boy's life had been a blood clot that had acted as a cork where the knife had penetrated his heart. The clot prevented the blood from gushing out of the heart.

The doctor said several times that it had been the blood clot that had miraculously saved the boy's life. We believe in miracles. We have no hesitation in praying for one. God does answer prayer.

Sunday mornings at Joy are refreshed through prayer. We have prayer teams who are present for each worship service. They pray for the worship service, for all the leaders, for the pastors, Sunday school teachers, ushers, greeters, and for all others who are serving in various capacities. At the end of every worship service, we announce publicly that if anyone would like to share in a time of prayer, a prayer team is present in the chapel. We have many who come for prayer who are ill or have a loved one who is ill, and some who are preparing to go to the doctor or the hospital. We also welcome a large number of people who have emotional or spiritual needs.

We also encourage prayers of thanksgiving. People who are celebrating positive events, birthdays, and anniversaries also come to pray. We encourage people to "pray without ceasing." A very visible prayer ministry is a living testimony to what we believe God can do and is doing through prayer.

The language of prayer is crucial. We try to reimagine such language. So often prayer has been rooted and grounded in Elizabethan nomenclature—words and images that were meaningful in another time but that clash with today's culture. We encourage people to speak the language in their hearts. We advise seekers to call upon God out of who they are and through what they are experiencing. We continue to experiment with new forms and languages.

Several major initiatives can arise from a dynamic and public prayer ministry. I highlight eight of them:

1. *Prayer chains.* The prayer chains consist of persons who communicate to another person in the telephone chain an important (sometimes urgent) request. After receiving the call, a person on the prayer chain calls the next person on the list with the request and then, after the call, prays for the

request. Usually a single chain is not longer than twelve to twenty people.

Prayer chains are very effective and rather easy to organize. One great benefit is the involvement of a large number of members. Confidentiality is to be maintained at all times. That is not difficult when people are praying for one another.

2. *Prayer groups.* The Joy prayer groups are comprised of two different types of groups: (a) *small prayer groups,* or what we often refer to as the prayer cells, and (b) *corporate prayer meetings.*

The prayer cells are small groups with an emphasis on prayer, both studying about prayer and actually praying. They usually meet in homes. These groups are usually small, from three to about ten members. If they become larger than ten, they usually divide into two or more smaller groups.

3. *Intercessory prayer group.* This is a group of people from all over the world who feel called by God to pray for others. The members of this group are bound together through a prayer newsletter and a prayer calendar. The local intercessors are called upon to pray for a variety of different functions, such as church services, youth meetings, pastors, and speaking engagements.

Silent intercessory prayer teams are being developed. In this ministry persons will pray silently during an activity of the church (such as a worship service or a class).

4. *College of Prayer.* Exciting opportunities to learn more about prayer are found in the College of Prayer. The College of Prayer will train the people who want to be a part of the prayer ministry. A variety of excellent courses will encourage people to spend more time in prayer. For those who want to be intentional in their prayer courses, one of three degree programs may be of interest.

The College of Prayer is offering nearly fifty classes during each academic year. Bachelor's, master's, and doctor's certificates of prayer are offered for those who want to pursue a serious study in prayer and become involved in the prayer ministry.

5. *Prayer teams.* Prayer team members pray for the pastors before church services begin on Saturday evening or Sunday morning and evening. They also pray with anyone who comes to church and seeks prayer support. The prayer team ministry offers an excellent opportunity to put prayer learning into actual practice by praying for people's needs. Prayer teams also visit people in hospitals and nursing homes, shut-ins, and those who have recently had loved ones die.

6. *Twenty-four-hour prayer telephone line.* Anyone who has a prayer concern can call the church prayer line and request prayer by one of Joy's trained telephone intercessors. This ministry also offers a great opportunity for people to put into practice God-given prayer gifts.

7. *Prayer retreats.* A number of prayer retreats are scheduled for every year to help people learn more about prayer and to pray. A retreat is used to build team spirit and to spend time developing listening and dialogue skills with God.

8. *Prayer partners.* The prayer ministry of Joy encourages all members of the church, starting with the leadership, to establish prayer partnerships. Each member is encouraged to link up with another person and regularly exchange prayer needs and requests, then take time to pray together about those needs. These prayer partnerships include long-distance national and international prayer partners in addition to prayer partners within the immediate congregation.

It might not be practical for you to implement plans in your congregation immediately for eight distinct prayer ministries. You are encouraged instead to select one or two of the prayer ministries you think might best suit your congregation at this time. You may target other parts for the future. Start where the ministry of prayer has a fit, in whatever way God leads you. The leaders show the way with a good example. Your church will do as your leaders do.

▼   LIST YOUR KEY DISCOVERIES   ▼

We at Joy believe that prayer has the power to change the world. God indeed does answer prayer. Prayer changes each person who prays and prayer can transform a congregation, then a community. I truly believe God gave us this new perspective on our vision to help all persons know that Jesus is Lord. There is no doubt it has made a profound difference in our ministry.

Reflect on the practice of prayer in your congregation. Write out in a sentence or two how you are training people to pray. Then, perhaps from key discoveries in this chapter, write down two ways that you will improve the prayer ministries of your church.

_____

_____

_____

_____

For more information about the prayer ministry or the prayer curriculum that we use, please write or call:

Community Church of Joy
21000 North 75th Avenue
Glendale, AZ 85308
602-938-1460

6 INNOVATIONS IN CHURCH STRUCTURE

When I arrived at Joy, two different groups jockeyed for control of the church council. One of these groups endorsed change, the other fought strenuously against it. One welcomed innovation with support and encouragement, the other wanted only to maintain the status quo.

After a couple of years in Phoenix, I unintentionally drove away some of the worst critics. As for the others, their council terms came to an end, and we elected people who shared a dynamic vision. I became very proactive with the nominating committee, recommending people who were forward looking and action-oriented. I expected that with a much different group of council members we could begin to function much more excellently, efficiently, and effectively. How wrong I was.

At the time, I was obviously the only staff member at Joy. The council was not unlike many leadership groups in similar situations. The members expected me to take care of just about everything. I led the worship, visited the sick, recruited the new members, recruited and trained the Sunday school teachers, supervised the youth group, raised the money, and in my spare time worked on a cure for cancer.

Since I was the only person around the church much of the time, I responded to every emergency. At times I ended up scrubbing floors, cleaning up after overflowing toilets, digging trenches for electrical work, cleaning away brush and weeds from the site, laying sod, and printing bulletins. Whatever needed to be done, I was the only one nominated to do it.

The church council was organized so that each person had oversight for a specific ministry. Youth, education, music, finance, worship, and other areas had council leaders. Often people were asked to lead in areas in which they had no interest, but they accepted the job out of a sense of duty. Consequently, they gave little creative effort to the ministry, for they had already said they had no interest in it.

 KEY DISCOVERY: An innovative organization produces an innovative operation.

God has shown me that I should not call anyone profane or unclean.
—Acts 10:28

By and large the council members viewed themselves as the officials in charge of managing a ministry, and they viewed me as the servant hired to carry out the actual work. I had a dozen or so supervisors, each committed to making sure that I expended plenty of time and energy to his or her specific charge.

We had no job descriptions. This meant that most of the council members had little clue as to what they were to be doing. We had no training procedures, no mission statement, no consistent strategy. Almost everything we did was reactive.

Our council meetings always began the same way. The treasurer would rise and paint a picture of gloom and doom: We have no money, therefore we cannot spend any money; no one should even think about suggesting something with a price tag. When he finished, it would be my turn to give the pastor's report. The climate by then was not very hospitable for talk about a daring, expanding ministry.

The church council members were operating in a system that no longer worked. Some were in the wrong positions, to be sure, but even those who were in the right places often felt frustrated and inadequate. Failure was the prevailing sentiment, especially since the programs had names but not much activity.

I did the best I could do with the council members. I had lunch with them, supported and encouraged them as persons and as elected leaders. I trained all of them in leadership and ministry. In spite of all my efforts, council meetings often dragged on for four hours or more, exhausting each of us. We headed for home discouraged and frustrated.

I dreamed of the day when we could hire a highly motivated staff. I wanted to bring aboard people who could give their total attention and energy to specific areas of ministry. I believe that the only way a church can ever move ahead in a dynamic way is by bringing together the most gifted, Christ-centered, and competent staff people it can find. The existing management system at Joy would never work. We were destined to find the wrong people for the wrong job in the wrong system.

Our mission statement and visioning process had been the beginning of a new day. In that document we had put together a staffing plan for the next decade. We started very modestly, with the addition of two part-time persons. We payed them almost nothing, but promised them opportunities to grow the ministry and the job.

Almost overnight we noticed a dramatic difference. As paid staff, these people suddenly sensed an endorsement and developed a passion for a specific ministry. I had not seen this before. They were willing to be trained and empowered. Their excitement about being a part of a ministry team was contagious throughout all parts of the congregation.

The entire climate changed. We soon added several more part-time staff members. Some council members were not pleased with this development. In fact, some of them fought each new staff person we hired. They objected to staff members being paid while they as council members were giving their time for nothing. No change had an easy birth when we were still functioning within an unworkable system.

Creating Ministry Teams

As time progressed, the staff members we hired at low wages began adding more time, some becoming quarter-time or half-time, and some eventually became full-time. We never had enough money for these staff members, and no church ever will, but we have never let the lack of money determine our decisions to be in ministry so that all may know Jesus Christ. Always believing that an outstanding staff person would pay for herself or himself very soon, we almost always hired someone part-time at first. Then, if the person was doing superior work, the finances would soon be present to move her or him into full-time work.

I believed that a ministry team was the solution. *We were much better together than we ever would have been alone.* Restructuring meant reimagining with a staff team how the congregation *could* be and then preparing a plan to carry this dream forward. I looked for people with a passion and a heart for ministry. I sought those who not only were open to consistent learning but also invested themselves in growth. We wanted those who would support and promote our vision.

I made many mistakes in these early years. I often asked people to join our staff based on my own intuition or casual impressions rather than following a comprehensive hiring strategy. I often guessed wrong. Since that time, we have developed a rather intensive and exhaustive interview and selection process.

My early strategy for accomplishing our vision was to find the best possible staff persons I could find. Many of them came from within. All of us joined together to become a team. My assumption was that when we had staff people in place, the council members elected to various positions might be greatly relieved. The council member would no longer have to worry so much about the specific ministry, because the staff members would bear the responsibility for daily, ongoing effectiveness. I was wrong again when it came to controllers.

 KEY DISCOVERY: Teamwork is an essential key to effectiveness in ministry.

A power struggle began almost immediately between a council member and a staff member. Would the council member elected to oversee youth ministry be in charge, or would the youth director have authority? Compromise was hard to achieve. I attempted to find ways to bring about peace and harmony—to build bridges—but the tension never quite went away. It is a daunting task in an organization to try to reallocate and distribute the power and control.

Another problem came with accelerating growth. As new staff persons came on board, as the organization became more complex, the council members often found themselves out-of-touch with the day-to-day ministry. They knew less and less about what was going on. I received many phone calls from council members who wanted to know more about what was happening. We went from one council meeting per month to two so that we could keep in better touch, but the faster events moved, the less the council could be involved. This communication gap was a source of inevitable conflict.

A New Structure

The situation finally changed when we elected a few more people from the corporate world to the church council. Many of them were steeped in systems in which the governing board had nothing at all to do with administration and management. The board set the policy, and the staff carried out the management.

Some of our business leaders finally decided that we needed to create an entirely new structure. If we were to move into the future, we could not continue operating the way we had been doing in the past. We were convinced that the failures we encountered were not failures of people but of the system. We had outstanding people trying to lead an antiquated system.

 KEY DISCOVERY: The church staff (including the pastor) is called, not to do the work of ministry, but to manage it.

From these deliberations came a rather radical proposal. We made the decision to *become a staff-led church rather than a council-led organization.* A task force decided that the most important role of the governing body was to select the key staff members and then to let the staff organize and move as they saw fit. The council would deal with policy and vision. The staff would organize and manage the ministry.

Staff members were not being called to do the work so much as to manage the work. We knew from the beginning that we would never be able to afford enough staff to do all the ministry. We needed to find people who were willing to equip others, to give away the ministry and their own security. Each year we ask our staff members, What have you given away to others? Who have you trained?

Shrink the Council

We also decided that those who were on staff and elected to the church council had to not only talk the Christian life but also live it. This conclusion resulted in five guidelines.

We agreed that all of our leaders must covenant to live these principles before they could be selected: (1) regular worship, (2) daily prayer and Bible reading, (3) constant growth through training and workshops, (4) tithing, and (5) being a part of an outreach mission.

We believed that people who adhered to such guidelines for Christian living would be transformed by the power of Jesus Christ. These were the kind of leaders we needed: people who were transformed. At one time we had had council members who neither were in worship with us often nor gave. No longer would we name such persons as leaders. We were convinced that Christian character was more important than credentials.

Having implemented these changes, we believed we had a system that would work. Council leaders would approve policy and vision; the staff would manage the ministry. During the period of transition we encountered much confusion. Church council members still tried to micromanage. We were trying to become a twenty-first-century church with a mid-twentieth-century management structure. We knew it was not working, but we did not know where to go from there.

 KEY DISCOVERY: A church is organized either to grow or to decline.

Finally, again led by some corporate leaders, we decided to *phase out the church council system and create a board of directors.* We created an entirely new structure, much like that of a business organization in which the board sets policy and then delegates all management and administration responsibilities to the staff.

This turned out to be the best decision we ever made in the area of structure. The transition from the church council to a board of directors was not easy, for many people remembered yesterday. But finally, we shifted entirely to a new polity. What a benefit this has been for our church. Everything has changed. No longer do we have the conflict that characterized the previous system.

Church councils now appear to be a phenomenon of yesterday's church, in which elected leaders truly did represent the membership as a whole. Historically, church council members were neighbors, friends, or relatives of a large percentage of the whole congregation. They truly were representative of the church's membership and of the geographical area where they were located.

In larger churches, however, especially those representing today's culture, hardly anyone knows who is on the church council. Even fewer are concerned. Most council members tend to represent themselves, which is hardly representative government. Often it is the pastor or the staff who is most concerned about the church council's makeup. No one else seems to pay much attention.

Additional problems surface when many church council members come to their positions with specific personal agendas. They want to see some area of ministry expanded, they want to promote or demote a particular staff person, they want to change some directions. If the staff leaders agree with this agenda, it can work smoothly. If the staff is on a different track, idiosyncratic conflict is inevitable. When council members are elected to oversee specific ministries for which they most naturally feel ownership and responsibility, problems are almost sure to incite polarization. Staff members are often caught in no-win situations.

We elect our board of directors for at-large positions. No one member of the board has program responsibility. We have just seven members, following Lyle Schaller's admonition that the larger a church becomes, the smaller the governing body should be. Most of these seven have considerable experience in management and leadership.

They have been invaluable in helping us with vision and direction.

Members of our board of directors serve two-year terms and can serve up to three terms. After six years they retire from the board. This gives us opportunity to be infused constantly with new leadership and vision for our future.

The board selects its own president, vice president, and treasurer. These positions are created mostly for legal and corporate reasons. The actual management of the ministry is done by the staff. As chief of staff, I consistently bring training and clarification to the board regarding its role and what decisions it needs to make.

We no longer hold elections. A nominating committee consisting of the senior pastor, the administrator, and members of the board prepares a new slate of board members for the coming year. These are brought to the congregation for *confirmation*. With the specific qualifications we have established for board members, it is no longer prudent to have nominations from the floor. We take time to check out all nominees to see if they have met the five guidelines named above. The nominating committee interviews all prospective board members, finds if they support the vision of the church and meet the standards, and then it makes recommendations. This careful process reduces the possibility of confirming someone who might wish to disrupt or derail our ministry, which is something we have experienced in our early years.

 KEY DISCOVERY: Always remember that the real business of the church is people—not policies, procedures, or politics.

I learned early that what happens at the beginning of a meeting affects the entire remainder of the meeting. When the treasurer begins the meeting with financial news, it influences the rest of the evening. When the meeting is in a formal space, with people sitting around tables, people will respond in more predictable, structured ways.

We have discovered that the key to working with a board of directors (or a church council) is to build trusting and caring relationships. All vision and strategy flow from those relationships. Lyle Schaller taught me that the most important dimension of church leadership is trust, which leads to respect. The spiritual climate is vital to building that trust and respect.

We normally meet in the homes of our board members. There we have a very informal atmosphere, where we are more a small group than a board. Kennon Callahan observes that most people want community rather than committees; so our board tries to become a community.

We begin our meetings by "checking in." We learn about some of the struggles or joys each of us has experienced since we were last together. We spend considerable time praying for one another. Very often each of us is facing some stress or even a crisis. Prayer and listening attend to these needs right at the beginning. Often the first hour of the meeting (beginning at 7:00 P.M.) is devoted to prayer and conversation.

By the time we begin the business, we move very quickly. Often the agenda takes no more than one-half hour. We always end our meetings by 9:00. Everyone goes home encouraged and refreshed. This is so much more satisfying than going home angry or frustrated that things are wrong with the congregation.

Congregational meetings also have changed dramatically. We have two such meetings each year, held on a Sunday morning after the 11:30 worship service. The first is held on the third Sunday in February in order to present the end-of-the-year reports. The second is in November in order to present the budget and confirm the board of directors.

Two weeks in advance of each meeting we have open forums on Sunday morning. This gives people an opportunity to discuss and debate the various recommendations and decisions presented. When the actual congregational meeting is held, however, the purpose is only to vote. No discussion except for explanation takes place at that time. Most meetings take twenty minutes. The days of the four-hour annual meeting are over.

In most congregations the church councils and boards spend huge amounts of valuable time and energy pretending that they are doing management. The staff spends its time doing ministry. We think this is a poor reflection of the New Testament patterns for ministry, and it violates our common sense. We think that the staff is called to do the management. We have the calling, the time, the expertise, the team cohesiveness to envision, manage, organize, and train. We also believe that the members of our congregation are called to ministry, to be in mission. Staff does the management, and laity does the ministry.

For much of my ministry the monthly meeting of the church council was the worst night of my month. I got sick before the meeting, and I was often even sicker after it. Large numbers of Christian leaders have suffered incessant anguish, pain, and frustration over governance structures that may only have worked when the church was in charge of the village culture. Today, I look forward to the board of directors' monthly meetings, because I know that we are organized to envision what God wants for us.

LIST YOUR KEY DISCOVERIES

Reflect on ways to reengineer the structure of your church so that your congregation can move from gridlock to effectiveness. Think of ways that you might move more quickly, with much greater confidence than ever before. A church is far more than its structure, but structure is hardly unimportant. A dysfunctional structure can paralyze a church.

CHAPTER 7 CIRCLE OF FULFILLMENT

Our vision at Joy is to help people discover a personal relationship with Jesus Christ and enthusiastically become responsible members of the church. As I mentioned in chapter 2, it used to be the case that most visitors to Lutheran congregations were lifelong Lutherans. The way of accepting such people was through a letter of transfer. Most of the time the classes for new members were only for those who were not of Lutheran or Christian background. Those numbers were usually small. Nearly identical practices can be found in other long-established denominations.

At Joy most of the people coming into membership come with little or no church background. They have hardly an echo of our language, to quote Alan Walker, not even an "echo of an echo of an echo" (Walker, 29-30). At least 70 percent of new people coming to Joy are unchurched. The majority are called baby boomers, those born between 1946 and 1964.

Lyle Schaller highlights how different those people born after World War II are from those born before 1940. The concepts of the Depression or the Big War simply do not exert any influence on those born after World War II. Powerful forces have given shape to this new generation.

In studying the people we are reaching, some of the basic characteristics of this age-group include the following:

Their *culture* has been shaped by station wagons, hula hoops, Disneyland, McDonald's, suburbs, health clubs, TV, movies, and numerous other entertainment options.

Formative events in their lives include civil defense drills, bomb shelters, the Cuban missile crisis, the assassinations of John Kennedy, Bobby Kennedy, and Martin Luther King Jr., civil rights riots, the Vietnam war, Watergate, OPEC, the destruction of the immediate family unit (50 percent of parents divorce), the advent of (but looming threats to) mass affluence. Children of divorced boomers rarely see their fathers.

The *motto* of an unchurched seeker tends to be "Live for today, not for tomorrow."

90 percent are high school graduates.
22 percent are college graduates.
80 percent think often about money.
60 percent worry about money.
80 percent of boomer women work outside the home.

They
- are fiercely independent and self-reliant.
- blame failures on society, not individuals.
- trust only themselves.
- distrust political parties, brand-name products, and things that have "deceived" them.
- are less likely to be committed to marriage (50 percent will divorce).
- are less likely to be committed to church or a denomination.
- view truth as relative.
- demand quality childcare.
- expect to change careers three times.
- have less leisure time than other Americans, and it continues to shrink.
- perceive church services to be boring, slow, and dull.

- perceive institutional church as being money-hungry.
- perceive church to be unfriendly, cliquish, irrelevant, and impractical.

How, then, is the church to respond to this generation? The old ways simply will not work, but hundreds of thousands of congregations have chosen not to act on this knowledge.

At Joy we have discovered that it is an enormous waste of talent and energy if we simply fill an auditorium without entering guests into a process toward doing ministry. There is a continuum along which we intentionally encourage and help this generation travel.

 KEY DISCOVERY: Growth must always be essential, never optional.

Grow in the grace and knowledge of our Lord and Savior Jesus Christ.

—2 Peter 3:18

Even though entertainment captures people's attention and holds it long enough so that we may share the good news of Jesus Christ, we do everything we can to help each person grow in a personal relationship with Jesus Christ and develop the practices that are expected of Christian disciples.

Circle of Fulfillment

If guests remain as spectators, on the fringe of the congregation, they will leave by the back door. The back door of so many larger churches can become an easy pathway to follow. Those who do not become a part of the ministry will most likely find the exit. While church observers such as Lyle Schaller say that every church is a revolving door, and at least 10 percent of the people are looking for some reason to leave, we want to connect with at least the other 90 percent. We encourage people to move from being uninvolved to being involved.

We call this growth process at Joy the *circle of fulfillment.* This is not a ladder. People are not climbing closer and closer to God, or to other wise persons higher up than them. A circle has a spirit of wholeness. It creates an image of people standing together hand in hand, learning and forming a community. If our new members experience the circle of Joy as a community, then we will help them discover the practices and disciplines of the church.

So many congregations believe that the way to bring people into ministry is to put them on committees. If we could change the world by committees, we would have shaped it up long ago. We have learned that there is often no *worse* way to excite new people about the church and the faith. Committees can often be caught up in the paralysis of analysis, not sure of why they exist. Committees were created to protect the status quo. Committees give staff members something abstract to supervise or influence.

People are looking for community, not committees. We want to build in our new members a sense of the whole community of faith. We desire that they experience the love and grace of God and then move into the ministry. Every person is a minister; every minister has a mission. This inclusivity is a part of a growing, dynamic process rather than the regulatory purpose committees assign to themselves.

Four commitments mark our circle of fulfillment. Each of these is an essential part of the process of making disciples.

The first is *a commitment to membership.* For those who are thinking about making this first commitment, we offer an orientation class in which we tell the story of Joy, the beliefs of Joy, the purpose and strategy of Joy, and what membership at Joy entails. Every person who comes to Joy is encouraged to follow along the circle at least this far.

At the end of the committment class we ask each person who is serious about becoming a member to sign a covenant. God has made a covenant with us, so we ask people to also sign a covenant.

My Commitment to Membership

Acknowledging Jesus as my Friend, Savior and Lord and acknowledging my agreement with the beliefs and strategy of Joy, I enthusiastically commit myself to membership at Joy. As a member I will do the following:

1. I will uphold the vision of Joy
   - by praying for the staff of Joy.
   - by praying for the family of Joy.
   - by praying for the leaders of Joy.
2. I will share in the mission of Joy
   - by praying for Joy's growth.
   - by inviting the unchurched to attend.
   - by lovingly welcoming those who attend.
3. I will serve in the ministry of Joy
   - by cultivating a serving heart.
   - by discovering my God-given gifts and talents.
   - by plugging into an area of service and mission.
4. I will support the mission of Joy
   - by attending worship regularly.
   - by growing in my faith.
   - by investing a portion of my resources regularly.

The second part of the circle of fulfillment is called *discovering maturity*. Our focus for this is spiritual maturity, Bible study, prayer, a design for living, and giving. We encourage everyone participating to join one of the small groups at Joy. Again we ask for a further commitment.

My Commitment to Maturity

Acknowledging my desire to grow in the grace of Jesus Christ through the ministry of Joy, I enthusiastically commit myself to do the following:

1. I will seek to spend daily quiet time in prayer and study of God's Word.

2. I will faithfully participate in a small group or class on a regular basis.

3. I will support the church financially by giving of my tithe, or I will commit to move toward a tithe in the near future.

The third part of the circle of fulfillment has to do with discovering the gifts of people. We communicate with great enthusiasm that each person is incredibly gifted by God. Our purpose is to help people become aware of these gifts.

We call this process *discovering ministry*. We use some evaluation tools to help people discover their gifts and then talk about how these might be used in the church, the community, and the world. We look at the heartbeats of people, their personalities, their temperaments, and we see how God has prepared each of us for ministry. At the end, as before, we ask for another commitment.

My Ministry Covenant

Having committed myself to membership and the habits essential for spiritual maturity, and agreeing with Joy's Ministry Statement, I commit myself to do the following:

1. I will seek to discover my unique shape for ministry and serve in the area that best expresses what God made me to be.

2. I will demonstrate a servant's heart by serving in the secondary ministries as the Body of Christ needs me.
3. I will cooperate with other ministries and place the greater good of the whole Body over the needs of my ministry.

The signed covenant asserts, "This certifies that you are a commissioned minister of Jesus Christ, through Community Church of Joy, and are entrusted with the related responsibilities and privileges."

The fourth part of the circle of fulfillment focuses outward, on our ministry to the world. This is called *discovering missions.* We discuss principles of effective witnessing and how we can give away our faith. We encourage every person to have a mission. We conclude by expending effort in equipping these leaders. We then ask them to sign a fourth covenant.

Mission Opportunities

I would like to be a part of reaching out with the gospel of Jesus Christ in our community.
• We list various outreach ministries of Joy.
• We ask for volunteers in the various holiday missions.
• We invite people to be a part of short-term missions.
• We highlight the opportunities for international outreach.

As a devoted follower of Jesus Christ and as a leader of Community Church of Joy, I commit to the following:
• Regular worship
• A daily prayer life
• Growing in my faith
• Giving 10 percent of my income back to God
• Sharing my faith with others through my lifestyle
• Upholding the mission, strategy, and values of Joy

Imagineering for Small Groups

Because so many of our guests need to find a community rather than committees, we have strongly emphasized the small group movement at Joy. We offer friendship groups, support groups, growth groups, activity groups, and prayer groups. Large numbers of people participate. The larger we become, the smaller we must be.

Some of the specific resources we have developed for small groups are described in the section that follows.

Adult Education

To help adults to keep on growing, we offer the Academy of Christian Growth. Opportunities for growth are divided into three categories: faith, life, and ministry.

Faith: Examples of the classes that help one discover and grow in one's faith and accept the promises of faith for oneself include "Discover the Bible," "Profiles in Christian Ideals," "Old Testament," "Four Gospels—One Message," and "Amazing Grace."

Life: Examples of growth opportunities in this dimension include classes in marriage, parenting, finances, stress, "Significantly Single," and more, which help one live life to the fullest potential within God's plan for one's life. Some of the classes for life are "Faith and Finances," "Search for Significance," "Active Parenting," "Conflict Resolutions," and "Power Life."

Ministry: Aspects of ministry such as leadership, service, outreach, and mission are taught through "How to Give Away Our Faith," "Living Proof," and "Friends of Joy."

Within each of these areas, many choices are possible according to individual need and background. Also, credits can be earned toward a Christian Growth Award, which honors those dedicated to growth in relationships with Christ, family, and community.

Small Groups

Small groups are a substantial part of the Christian growth circle. Most of us had a small group of friends in school. These were the friends we dreamed with and cried with. This kind of friendship group provided a sense of community.

At Community Church of Joy we want to provide similar types of friendship-based small groups. Our small groups consist of ten to fourteen people who get together regularly on a weekly or biweekly basis. They meet in someone's home or in a restaurant or at church for growth through study, fellowship, prayer, support, and service. Some groups use the Bible as text. Other groups use a practical Christianity book to focus on family, marriage, career, stress, finances, women's issues or men's issues, grief, eating disorders, physical challenges, divorce recovery, anger, staying sober, aging, and more.

New groups are beginning continuously. Most small groups commit to meet for six to eight weeks and then reevaluate continuation. Small group growth is one of the most substantial growth opportunities available today in the Christian church.

The vision of Joy is to reach people with the gospel of Jesus Christ—we do that through entertainment evangelism—*and* to help them become responsible members of his church. Joy's growth opportunities are designed to help people, particularly the many new people who have had little or no prior church involvement, to move into a life of Christian discipleship. Entertainment evangelism has permitted a steady and healthy flow of growth.

People move from membership to maturity to ministry to mission. The growth circle can also be reversed. As people become immersed in mission, they are then brought back to the importance of ministry. Those in mission and ministry develop a maturity by their experience. All of this gives meaning to membership.

Children's Ministry

Creativity and innovation define our children's growth cycle. Many weekends, Joy launches a children's event with a power-packed musical, a dramatic presentation that we call *Bossolopolis*. This entertaining weekly production captures children's imaginations long enough to convey biblical truths that develop Christian behavior and values.

Following *Bossolopolis*, children break into age-groups with eight to fifteen participants for interactive learning. Each age-group has trained and turned-on teachers focusing on expressing Christ's unconditional, nonjudgmental love through informational and inspirational activities, Bible stories, and prayer time.

Weekday growth for children includes "I Am Special," a program for two- to five-year-olds, which builds a child's God-centered esteem and worth. For six- to nine-year-olds there is a "Joy Club," where high-energy activities help children develop a spirit of cooperativeness and improve their relational skills. The eight- to ten-year-olds have musical theater. Finally, the ten- to eleven-year-olds focus on developing leadership skills and Christian character as they are taken beyond the facts of life into a biblical, relevant application of Christ-centered values and ideals. We choose to believe that all children are filled with promising possibilities.

Teens

Teen growth is one of the highest priorities of our congregation. The teenage circle of fulfillment has "Five Big Gs."

1. *Grace:* Personally understanding the grace of God and trusting that Jesus Christ is Lord and Savior.
2. *Growth:* Committing to spiritual growth and living out a pattern of life changes.
3. *Group:* Committing to a small group of believers that pursues maturity and community involvement.
4. *Gifts:* Learning to express God-given gifts as a servant of Christ.
5. *Giving:* Giving to the church by owning responsibility and taking part in God's mission.

The strategy for this growth has seven steps:

1. *Integrity Friendship:* The process begins as we challenge our core students to "build relational bridges" with their non-Christian friends.
2. *Verbal Witness:* After building a credible friendship with their non-Christian friends we teach our core students to look for opportunities, in various ways, to explain and discuss their relationship with Christ.
3. *Evangelistic Events* (Providing a Service for Seekers): Outreach events are designed to nurture a student's spiritual interest by introducing him or her to the message of Christ in a contemporary and relevant way. Outreach events are intended to be used as tools by our core teens in reaching their non-Christian friends. They are designed to be supplements to their ongoing witness.
4. *Spiritual Challenge:* At this stage of their friendship we teach our core students to ask pointed questions that intentionally challenge their friends to consider the claims of Christ. We believe that once a seeker has spent time listening to God's Word and observing devoted Christian students, the seeker will discover through the conviction of the Holy Spirit his or her need for a personal relationship with Jesus Christ.

5. *Youth Worship and Teaching* (Integration into the Body): This is designed to support the believer's growing maturity on the trek toward full devotion to Christ. "Youth Today" provides believers with an opportunity to participate in corporate worship and to listen to expository Bible teaching.

6. *Action Groups:* Action groups provide a disciplined small group atmosphere that is triggered by a quality adult leader and four to six student members. From this small group come accountability, encouragement, and support, as well as biblical teaching through learning experiences.

7. *Ownership:* At this stage of students' spiritual development, they are taking active roles in service within the church. Both with their spiritual gifts and through tithing, they are owning their part of the Lord's work. A student now steps forward and takes the role of evangelist within his or her own circle of influence and thus begins a third spiritual generation. This occurs as the student takes his or her non-Christian friends through the same seven steps that he or she has already traveled.

▼ LIST YOUR KEY DISCOVERIES ▼

The circle of fulfillment works for Joy because it takes seriously the needs of unchurched persons. By moving persons around the circle, we are put in touch with persons who have not yet found Joy. Our growth circle never ends. Our Christian growth never ends. A ladder implies that once we have climbed to a certain height, we have arrived. A circle highlights our conviction that God is always bringing us through the process of growth. In addition, a circle demonstrates community. We do not grow alone, but hand in hand we press onward with like-minded strugglers. The growth circle has become a primary strategy for keeping our vision sharp and clear.

List what your congregation intentionally does to develop Christian practices and draw persons into ministry and mission. What one new thing would you like to do, starting now?

_____

_____

_____

_____

8 TEACHING CONGREGATIONS

Loren Mead, in *The Once and Future Church*, asserts that one of the major shifts taking place in the church today is the move *from teaching seminaries to teaching congregations*. He suggests that teaching seminaries were the paradigm of the nineteenth and twentieth centuries, but teaching congregations will be at the center of church life in the twenty-first century.

This does not entirely take us by surprise. This characteristic of innovation was present when immigrant churches arrived in the colonies. Teaching churches are now necessary for the new waves of Asian immigrants, such as the Korean Methodists and Presbyterians who have started dozens of local seminaries *inside* congregations.

The shift has already been under way in earnest for the past quarter-century as we have entered this "in-between time." The first teaching church I attended was the Crystal Cathedral in the mid-1970s. At the time, I was particularly interested in youth work, evangelism, and worship. I sought every workshop I could find in these areas.

In addition, I also received in the various plenary sessions a short course in preaching, administration, lay ministry, education, and leadership. I found the opportunity of experiencing a teaching church to be of inestimable value in creating neccessary new structures and in implementing the vision that God had given our congregation.

Since that time I have attended almost every teaching church I have been able to find. Much of my learning and expanded vision has come through such events. Congregations such as Willow Creek Community Church, with Bill Hybels, and Saddleback Community Church in California, with Rick Warren, have been most influential.

 KEY DISCOVERY: The learning and discovery centers of the future are in teaching congregations.

"I will build my church."
—Matthew 16:18

Basically, a teaching church is a community of faith that has discovered some patterns and principles of effective ministry and that has a vision of sharing these insights with other congregations. For the most part, teaching churches self-select. No one from a bureaucratic structure sends accrediting teams and determines which congregations should become teachers and keepers of the Christian vision.

Rather, the desire to be a teaching church must come from within. The local leadership of a congregation must have a passion for the gospel and a passion to help other congregations do well. Teaching churches believe that God's power is unlimited. The goal is to help as many congregations as possible to thrive, to discover God's vision, and to maximize their potential.

The teaching church has discovered, much like the Israelites wandering in the wilderness, that if they hoard their resources, the bread of life, they will quickly spoil, like the Israelites' manna. The specific vision is to help congregations and leaders succeed. These churches are not threatened by other churches that are doing well. Quite the contrary, teaching churches perceive a cultural ecosystem: The better other churches do, the better it is for all churches.

To become a teaching church is often a costly venture. In the initial years the financial cost is always higher than the return. A strong dollar investment in the lives of other ministers and congregations is necessary for a teaching church. The cost is measured in more than financial terms. It takes time, energy, and intentional development to be a teaching church. Sacrifices are necessary. Only those who are truly committed to sharing insights with other churches will continue this effort.

My own journey toward the concept of a teaching church took a rather convoluted path. Because of my own interest in evangelism, I was selected to be on the district evangelism committee early in my ministry at Joy.

Imagine the wisdom in choosing me. I had "succeeded" in downsizing our church from two hundred to one hundred in my first year and now was being asked to share my expertise and brilliance with the larger church. I quickly realized that many other people were struggling with evangelism challenges as well. It was comforting to realize that I was not the only one searching. Nevertheless, I realized early on that usually, in trying to figure out their mission, such judicatory committees produce much noise but little impact. Then, by the time they have a plan, their terms run out, and they move on to something else.

The year I was elected, for some reason or another, the evangelism committee had been given the assignment of planning the district convention. The convention was the focal event of the Lutheran congregations of the entire region. Several hundred pastors and lay leaders would be gathered together for three days each year.

I suggested that this convention might be a good opportunity for us to give a wider group of Lutherans an ample taste of the "teaching church" phenomenon. Since there were no such churches in Lutheran circles, I recommended that we invite Robert Schuller to come and speak to us. He could teach us some of the same principles that he teaches people who come to his teaching church conferences.

The evangelism committee agreed that this was an excellent idea. Since I had a prior relationship with Schuller, I was asked to issue the invitation. We also decided to mention in the preconvention publicity that we may not agree with everything that Schuller might say.

Such a disclaimer should not have been necessary. We often listen to people at such conventions with whom many in the group disagree. But we wanted to go the second mile in being sensitive to the reluctance that some would have. We wanted Schuller to challenge us, to help us look at a new vision, to express new ideas, and to instill us with new passion for the unchurched.

Soon after the publicity was distributed, resistance began forming around the judicatory. Nasty letters and phone calls rained in on the district office. Lobbying began in earnest to protest this invitation to Robert Schuller. This was the same judicatory that had had no trouble at all inviting non-Christians to address the convention. We listened respectfully. We might have had little trouble with radical expressions from the left, but by no means did many of our pastors want to listen to anyone who was perceived as an evangelical or as part of the "church growth" movement—especially Robert Schuller, who also gets his dose of criticism from evangelicals who think that he has sold out to the culture.

As the convention drew nearer, people threatened protests, marches, even public demonstrations. A few days before the convention the bishop called me and told me that there was so much opposition that it threatened the life of the convention itself. He told me it was necessary to withdraw our invitation to Robert Schuller. I told the bishop that it was not up to me to carry out this rejection. I strongly disagreed with the action. If the bishop needed to do this, then he should make the call himself. The bishop called Robert Schuller and told him we did not want him to come.

Of course the press had a field day with this turn of events. Our district now had become a prime example of a group that, while intoning a message of inclusivity and respect for others, was really intolerant and narrow-minded. I realized that fundamentalism was alive on the left and the right and that the polarization was deadly to reaching people with the gospel.

I learned another valuable lesson in this experience: Affirmation from a church judicatory to color outside the lines often comes at a high price. It is much easier to ask for forgiveness than for permission.

I ascertained that the place for imagination and creativity is not in the bureaucracy, inside the structures created by people who have already retired, but in the congregation. I learned again one of the major reasons why teaching churches have come into existence: Denominations and judicatories are closed systems that exist to secure the futures of their managers.

I became convinced that I should be a part of an effort to help create a teaching church. I wanted to focus on evangelism, on new forms of worship, on creative programming, and on reaching the unchurched. I did not want to try to struggle through the maze of red tape and the political posturing or ambitions of the managers in a bureaucracy.

Ironically, soon after the invitation to Robert Schuller was withdrawn, the office of the bishop who withdrew it called me and offered our church $5,000 to have an evangelism conference of our own. The district could not sponsor such an effort because of a firestorm of criticism, but the bishop encouraged us to do it independently.

We agreed to have an evangelism conference, and since Joy still only had limited facilities, filled with children from 6:00 in the morning to 6:00 at night, we partnered with Dick Hamlin at Shepherd of the Valley Lutheran Church in Phoenix.

At our first conference we invited Robert Schuller and Lyle Schaller. Again we were vociferously attacked by various forces throughout the district, but this time they had no vote. We eventually sponsored four of these conferences. All of them were well attended and brought together people who were vitally interested in evangelism and not averse to new ways of finding and growing disciples of Jesus Christ.

 KEY DISCOVERY: Sharing breakthrough discoveries helps everybody win.

Eventually we had sufficient space at Joy to host conferences and become a teaching church. Since that time, Prince of Peace Lutheran Church has emerged as another teaching church in our denomination. And the denominational systems are taking notice, even as new associations, such as Leadership Network, develop the concept and build the relationships that will support innovative congregations.

Some of the workshops presented at a recent conference included "Preaching to the Unchurched," "Marketing the Mission," and "Growing Through Small Groups."

At another recent conference some of the plenary sessions covered the following topics:

Worship as Evangelism: Practical suggestions on how to make liturgical worship more visitor-friendly, including ideas on how to design a contemporary, outreach-oriented service.

How to Reach Secular People: An analysis of culture and the various models used to make an impact on a secular world for Christ.

Entertainment Evangelism: A look at one of our culture's top industries and how it affects our presentation of the gospel.

How to Grow a Church: Seven Practical Keys.

Reaching the Baby Boom Generation: A character study of the members of the largest generation in the history of our country, along with practical ideas on how to reach them.

 KEY DISCOVERY: One person with a dream can make a tremendous impact.

Two narratives highlight the impact of a teaching church. When I spoke in England, a young pastor from Strasbourg, France, was present. He was very excited about what he heard. We invited him to come to our conference in Phoenix to study more closely the principles of evangelism and church growth. He accepted the invitation and came to a teaching event. While he was at Joy, he began to create his own vision of a ministry that he could lead in France. Shortly after he returned home, the Lutheran bishop of his area called all the pastors together and shared with them the sad story of St. Nicholas Lutheran Church in Strasbourg.

At one time St. Nicholas had been one of the great cathedral churches of Europe. John Calvin had been one of its pastors, and Martin Luther had preached from its pulpit. In later years, Albert Schweitzer had been the musical curator. In the latter half of the twentieth century, however, the church had fallen on hard times.

Fewer and fewer people came to worship there, and about a generation ago the church had been closed. Only pigeons now inhabited this sacred space; they had left their marks. The bishop asked those present to submit any new ideas for restoring this historic church.

The pastor who had attended our conference stayed up all that night crafting a vision for St. Nicholas, including many of the principles he had learned at Joy. He saw this historic church becoming a haven for the unchurched, a place of hospitality and welcome for strangers. When he submitted his proposal, it was the only one the bishop received.

The bishop ran this proposal past all the bureaucratic structures and finally, with some reluctance, gave this eager young pastor permission to go ahead. He could now actually create a new vision for old St. Nicholas.

It took many weeks just to clean up the pigeon droppings. A building that has been neglected for a generation needs significant attention. All this reminded me a bit of arriving in Phoenix in 1978. At least we had no pigeons in the desert. We just had weeds.

Today, after being reopened for one year, the congregation has three hundred people worshiping on a Sunday. It now has the highest average attendance of any Protestant congregation in France. The pastor and lay leaders have a new vision for the unchurched, applying what they learned at our teaching church and others that they have attended. They have been empowered by seeing and touching and feeling the vision of another congregation.

A second story is equally instructive. A young man by the name of Enrique Estrada was working in a mission among the poor in Saltillo, Mexico. He invited us at Joy to participate in mission projects in his community. We did and shared a vision with him of reaching Mexico with the gospel and asked him to be a part of that vision.

He came to Joy to study our vision for a period of time. Then, before returning to Monterrey, Mexico, he created his own vision—one that focused on creating an evangelical church in that metropolitan area. His specific vision was to influence the leaders of Mexico so that Mexico could receive the good news.

After six months of training, we sent him to Monterrey and provided financial support for his mission. Through the ministry he has started there, he has touched hundreds of lives and connected with many leaders of the country. Among the people now in his congregation is the head of the Mexican stock exchange.

Many of the lay leaders of his congregation have also come to experience our teaching church. They are now implementing what they have learned, and the church is thriving and growing. We rejoice in one of the most dynamic ministries in Mexico.

Leaders Must Be Healed Before They Can Learn

Over the years of teaching leaders in other congregations, we have noticed that many people who attend come with broken spirits and exceedingly low morale. I was not really aware that the sense of frustration and pain was so commonplace, even though I have lived with much of the heartache myself. I had always assumed that no one else had endured quite the same struggles and hardships as we had at Joy. During our time together with pastors and lay leaders from all over the world, we have become far more conscious of how much hurt there is in the lives of church leaders.

 KEY DISCOVERY: The size of ministry pain is directly related to ministry gain.

Peter Steinke, in *The Lutheran* magazine, senses that there is more discouragement among pastors today than ever before. He quotes Roy Oswald from the Alban Institute, who asserts that roughly half of all clergy are either removed by their congregations or forced out within the first ten years of beginning parish ministry. Another 15 percent will be forced out during the last ten years of their ministries (Steinke, 8).

In a seminar he led at Community Church of Joy in 1996, William Easum, a prophetic contemporary church consultant, highlighted the following statistics from his research on clergy morale:

- 90 percent work more than forty-five hours a week; most work over sixty.

- 80 percent believe their ministry has adversely affected their family.
- 50 percent feel unable to meet the demands of the job.
- 90 percent say they are inadequately trained to cope with the ministry.
- 70 percent say they have a lower self-image than they did when they began in ministry.
- 40 percent say they have a serious conflict with a parishioner at least once a month.

At our teaching church workshops, we try to nurture hope and inspiration in those who are hurting. We share with them something of our painful journey, and we explain how we have been able to find a new sense of vision and hope.

We have a strong desire to help these leaders not only cope with opposition and conflict but also rediscover how exciting and dynamic ministry can be. We want to encourage, lift up, strengthen, and energize all who come. At the end of workshops, we offer personal prayer and blessing to all participants. Giving a blessing from one leader to another was crucial to the Old Testament communities. We need to do this for one another today. We seek to give such a blessing as a way of encouragement and empowerment. Also, a counselor is available throughout the conference to help attendees. The counselor's schedule is always booked solid. Church leaders today need to be offered not only information and strategy but also strong affirmation and hope.

 KEY DISCOVERY: Christians are called, not simply to be productive, but also to be reproductive.

Another reason why teaching churches have become so effective is the rapid trend in today's congregations toward hiring from within. Historically, most church staff members have been secured from seminaries, Bible colleges, and denominational training programs, too many of which have become graduate research schools.

We have moved from a paradigm of credentials to one of Christian character and competence. A local congregation nurtures someone with particular competence, commitment, and expertise and then hires that person. Christian education directors, volunteer coordinators, music directors, administrative assistants, directors of childcare, and many other positions have become commonplace.

Often these highly motivated people begin as volunteers and then are hired part-time. Eventually some of them become full-time. Most people hired from within have proven to be highly effective leaders for congregations.

The teaching church has become the educational experience of choice for large numbers of those hired from within. While they find it helpful to take various courses and educational offerings from academic institutions, what lay staff members find particularly empowering is learning from those who are doing much the same kind of ministry.

Invaluable information and support can be given to staff members by someone who has experience and expertise in a particular area of ministry. This is why teaching churches not only have large plenary sessions but offer numerous workshops as well. Hands-on assistance for specific ministries is one of the most valuable aspects of the workshops.

▼   LIST YOUR KEY DISCOVERIES   ▼

Teaching churches will become only more prominent. Loren Mead projects that they will become the major teaching centers of the twenty-first century. Already many of them are not only holding regular seminars but also publishing resources and producing services that can be shared with other congregations.

Think of competent leaders in your congregation. Which ones would you hire part-time to expand your staff? Reflect on what kind of knowledge or which skills are most needed in your congregation. Ponder honestly whether your church council prefers credentials or Christian character in leaders and staff members.

_____

_____

_____

_____

9 BRINGING THE GOOD NEWS TO LIFE

And the Word became flesh and lived among us.
—John 1:14*a*

The Theology of Entertainment Evangelism

In this incarnational reality, eternity and time, the divine and the human, salvation and creation are reconciled. We are no longer able to drive the wedge that parts the sacred and the secular. God has exclaimed God's rightful ownership over *everything* God has created.

Roger Fredrickson masterfully addresses this issue in his reflections on "the Word becoming flesh and dwelling among us. . . . Our only hope of sharing in the life of God is that the Word has really become flesh" (Fredrickson, 43-44).

A contemporary illustration of the gospel enfleshed may be found in the remarkable motion picture *Chariots of Fire*. Many Christians gave thanks to God when it was announced that this film had been chosen to receive the Academy Award for "Best Picture of the Year" in 1981. Who would have thought that a book with the dry, unappealing title of *The Official History of the Olympics* could become the basis for a thrilling, sensitive film? But this was the only book David Puttnam, an imaginative British motion picture producer, could find while he was rummaging through the big, empty house he had just rented in Los Angeles. Something clicked in Puttnam when he came upon the story of Eric Liddell, a gifted, dedicated Scottish runner, who had won the gold medal for the four-hundred-meter race in the 1924 Olympic games—a race in which he had never competed before. But this became his only opportunity to participate, after years of training, because he stubbornly refused to run trial heats for his regular one-hundred-meter distance, because the heats were on a Sunday. He would not yield to any pressure, including requests from the Prince of Wales.

As Puttnam read of Liddell's untarnished convictions, memories of his own childhood stirred—days of simpler values of right and wrong. Would people respond to this kind of story on film? It is always worth a try.

He gathered an amazing assortment of people to finance, produce, and distribute this picture: Dodi Fayed, an Arab shipping magnate; Alan Ladd Jr., a film distributor and the son of the actor Alan Ladd Sr.; officials from Twentieth Century Fox and Warner Brothers; Colin Welland, who had written the script for *Straw Dogs*; and a host of others. The picture was put together not to be a moral preachment, but because this was a good story to tell, and there was hope it might make some money.

Many of us know what happened. Running all through this "non-Christian" film was shining integrity and the winsome beauty of a quiet Christian witness that struck a responsive chord deep in our seeking, secular society, so jaded by sex and violence on the screen. People lined up at theaters all across the country and left grateful because they had seen and heard the truth. Surely, in some wondrous way, God had been at work in all this, right in the middle of an industry that multitudes of good people have written off as a hopeless, illiterate aspect of our culture. Dare we not believe that the Word had once again been revealed in flesh in a place where people least expected it?

We in the church, the "religious people," have taken far too lightly or turned our backs on great areas of real, fleshly life. We have said by our attitudes and lifestyles that the care of the earth, the intimacy of human sexuality, those artistic impulses expressed in painting and music and dance, the meaning and significance of work, and all the other great human ventures are really not our concern. We have more "spiritual" things to look after. So the false gods of the secularists, really demonic forces, move into the vacuum that we have left in vital areas, and life becomes cheap and vulgar, if not a barren wasteland of amusement.

The Orthodox Church in Russia during the rule of the czars is a tragic case in point. Rich and powerful, but callously unconcerned about injustice and poverty, its leaders debated the color of the clerical vestments while Kerensky and Lenin planned the Marxist revolution to "liberate the people." In our own country, vast church buildings, TV programs, and burgeoning statistics could blind us from accepting the reality and implications of the Word that has become flesh. But the presence of the living God in flesh opens endless possibilities for all creation.

In our time there are illustrations of the Word becoming flesh in many differing places: Bob Dylan writing songs that challenge our false values; John Perkins establishing an economic base for the powerless people of Mississippi; the dream of Millard Fuller, which has become Habitat for Humanity, personally owned housing giving new dignity to the desperately poor; Bill Leslie and his LaSalle Street congregation offering free legal help for the dispossessed of Cabrini Green in Chicago; Sojourners Community of Washington challenging the whole war-making madness of our times. These are just a few of those who "recover lost provinces, who reclaim the earth, in the name of Jesus who has come in flesh" (Fredrickson, 43-46).

The Practice of Entertainment Evangelism

In the form of a memory device, here are insights on practical applications and relevant implications of entertainment evangelism.

E   **E**nlist comments from community leaders on how to best understand the community's needs.

N   **N**otice what TV shows, movies, music, and dramatic events are attracting the attention of the people you are trying to reach.

T   **T**alk directly to people who don't go to church and ask them what it would take to get them involved.

E   **E**xamine what is working and what isn't working in your own congregation's outreach efforts.

R   **R**isk changes that will improve your ability to reach unchurched people.

T   **T**est your ideas and efforts by moving from discussion to action.

A   **A**ffirm strengths. Don't do everything, but do one or two things excellently.

I   **I**magine the new and different. This will break routine and boredom.

N   **N**ever quit. Persistence always pays.

M   **M**ove deliberately. Get rid of the lengthy committee processes and consensus criteria and *go for it!*

E   **E**xpect God's best. God wants every church to be a vibrant mission center.

N   **N**otice your market for ministries and programs. Offer the right things for the right people.

T   **T**rust God. Be bold. A fool for Christ is not a fool at all. The Bible labels fools as disciples or apostles or servants.

E   **E**ncourage creativity. Creativity is the prelude to breaking through barriers and solving difficult problems.

V   **V**alue biblical truths, creeds, and confessions that are foundational to the Christian faith.

A   **A**ccept differences. Allow God to use a variety of ways to reach each new generation with the gospel.

N   **N**urture Christian character. Rediscover what it means to live the Christian life and to grow in grace.

G   **G**raciously give. The greatest rewards come from giving.

E   **E**xercise all the spiritual gifts. The church functions best when the whole body is actively involved.

L   **L**ove without limits. Amaze people with love.

I   **I**nvite friends to church. The best way to win the world to Christ is through friendships.

S   **S**erve. "How may I be of service?" is the motto of healthy, happening churches.

M   **M**ake sure you don't miss the joy. Joy is clearly the identifiable mark of Christianity.

May these idea igniters be helpful to you as you live out the practical implications of entertainment evangelism.

The Motive of Entertainment Evangelism

After completing a series of lectures in America and Europe, I prayerfully pondered what I had learned. The discouragement of Christian pastors and leaders makes me heartsick. Many stand beside me with tears flooding from their eyes. It is true that many churches are in decline. Worship attendance is sinking, and the demographics in long-established denominations appear to be irreversible. Attitudes toward the church as a social participant are negative. *However*, the Bible assures us, "I will build my church, and the gates of Hades will not prevail against it" (Matt. 16:18).

I honestly believe that the best years for the church universal are still ahead of us. God is more aware than we are of the church's potential and possibilities. There is no reason to give up. *It is time to give out.* When we empty ourselves we are filled with fresh new wine.

As a new church is emerging, it will be filled afresh with the Holy Spirit. Many of the structures and styles will change, but one thing will never change—God's promise: "Jesus Christ is the same yesterday and today and forever" (Heb. 13:8).

A new day has dawned in the church. As we earnestly pray for the church, a new love and a new joy will fill our hearts. Our fears about the future security of our calling can be transformed by our sense that it is a humbling privilege to serve the church. Our fear and disappointment can only be driven out by the love and compassion for the church's mission that God nurtures within us.

Entertainment evangelism is one practical, simple, and intentionally visible tool that God uses to restore our compassion for a culture that is always losing its way. Mingling daily with ordinary people and rulers, Jesus operated, not in the shadows of the culture, but on the leading, dangerous edge of it. Because the edges of our present culture are reshaped so drastically by entertainment, let us find innovative, prayer-stretching ways to use entertainment to build strong churches, loving families, and healthy communities. Let's take a risk.

We need not be afraid of entertainment. I am convinced that the church can define and develop entertainment into a powerful resource for connecting the voice and the touch of God with our context and culture.

It is important to keep alert to the dangers of unproductive entertainment. Nevertheless, it would be much more dangerous and deadly for the church to ignore or even seek to destroy entertainment evangelism opportunities. As with all gifts and talents, we simply need to become wise stewards of entertainment tools.

One of the tremendous opportunities Christian ministers and church leaders have today is the opportunity of using our God-given imaginations to maximize entertainment evangelism. With all the technology and creative breakthroughs rushing through our world, we have a realistic hope that the whole world can be eternally changed.

Don't be amused. Take a risk that pre-Christians are waiting for your congregation to bring the gospel to life!

BIBLIOGRAPHY

Anderson, Leith. *A Church for the 21st Century*. Minneapolis: Bethany, 1992.

———. *Dying for Change*. Minneapolis: Bethany, 1990.

Anderson, Ray. *The Praxis of Pentecost*. Pasadena: Fuller Seminary, 1991.

Anfuso, Francis. *We've Got a Future*. Sierra Madre, Calif., 21st Century Ministries, 1989.

Applby, Jerry. *Missions Have Come Home to America*. Kansas City: Beacon Hill, 1986.

Arn, Win and Charles Arn. *The Master's Plan for Making Disciples*. Pasadena: Church Growth, 1982.

Arn, Win. *The Pastor's Manual for Effective Ministry*. Monrovia, Calif.: Church Growth, 1990.

Bakke, Ray. *The Urban Christian*. Downers Grove, Ill.: Intervarsity, 1987.

Barker, Joel. *Discovering the Future*. St. Paul: ILI, 1988.

———. *Future Edge*. New York: Morrow, 1992.

Barna, George. *The Frog in the Kettle*. Ventura, Calif.: Regal Books, 1990.

———. *The Power of Vision*. Ventura, Calif.: Regal Books, 1992.

———. *What Americans Believe*. Ventura, Calif.: Regal Books, 1991.

Basso, Bob with Judy Kosek. *This Job Should Be Fun!* Holbrook, Mass.: Bob Adams, 1991.

Bennis, Warren and Burt Nanus. *Leaders: The Strategy for Taking Charge*. New York: Harper & Row, 1985.

Bernstein, Carl. "The Leisure Empire." *Time* (24 December 1990): 56-59.

Bethel, Sheila Murray. *Making a Difference: Twelve Qualities That Make You a Leader*. New York: G. P. Putnam's Sons, 1990.

Blanchard, Kenneth and Norman Vincent Peale. *The Power of Ethical Management*. New York: Morrow, 1988.

Callahan, Kennon. *Twelve Keys to an Effective Church*. San Francisco: HarperSanFrancisco, 1983.

————. *Effective Church Leadership.* San Francisco: HarperSanFrancisco, 1990.

Campolo, Tony. *The Kingdom of God Is a Party.* Dallas: Word, 1990.

Carson, Ben with Cecil Murphey. *Think Big: Unleashing Your Potential for Excellence.* Grand Rapids: Zondervan, 1992.

Cho, Paul Yonggi. *The Fourth Dimension.* Seoul: Church Growth International, 1989.

Conn, Harvie. *Evangelism.* Grand Rapids: Academic Books, 1992.

Covey, Stephen. *Seven Habits of Highly Effective People.* New York: Simon and Schuster, 1989.

DePree, Max. *Leadership Is an Art.* New York: Dell, 1989.

Drucker, Peter. *Innovation and Entrepreneurship.* New York: Harper & Row, 1989.

————. "Marketing 101 for a Fast-Changing Decade." *Wall Street Journal,* November 20, 1990.

Engstrom, Ted, with Robert Larson. *Integrity.* Waco, Tex.: Word, 1987.

Exman, Gary. *Get Ready . . . Get Set . . . Grow!* Lima, Ohio: CSS, 1987.

Fox, Steve. "Ordway Musical Theater." *Minnesota Monthly Magazine* (fall, 1993).

Fredrickson, Roger. *The Communicator's Commentary: John.* Waco, Tex.: Word, 1985.

Friedman, Edwin. *Generation to Generation.* New York: Guilford, 1985.

Gallup, George Jr. and David Poling. *The Search for America's Faith.* Nashville: Abingdon, 1990.

Gibbs, Eddie. *Followed or Pushed?* London: MARC Europe, British Church Growth Association, 1987.

Greenleaf, Robert. *Servant Leadership.* New York: Paulist, 1987.

Haggai, John. *Lead On!* Waco: Word, 1986.

Hallesby, O., translated by Clarence Carlsen. *Prayer.* Minneapolis: Augsburg, 1931.

Helgeson, Sally. *The Female Advantage.* New York: Bantam, 1990.

Hillkirk, John. "Reengineering the Corporation." *USA Today,* Monday, November 8, 1993.

Hummel, Charles. "Tyranny of the Urgent." *The 2:7 Series, Course 1.* Colorado Springs: Navpress, 1974.

Hunter, George S. III. *How to Reach Secular People.* Nashville: Abingdon, 1992.

Hunter, Kent. *Moving the Church into Action.* St. Louis: Concordia, 1989.

————. *Foundations for Church Growth.* New Haven, Mo.: Leader, 1983.

Hybels, Bill. *Christians in the Marketplace.* Wheaton: Victor Books, 1988.

————. *Mastering Contemporary Preaching.* Portland: Multnomah, 1989.

Kallestad, Walt and Timothy Wright. "Worship as Evangelism." *Evangelism* (February 1991).

Kallestad, Walt. *Turning Financial Obstacles into Opportunities.* Burnsville, Minn.: Prince of Peace, 1987.

Keifert, Patrick. *Welcoming the Stranger.* Minneapolis: Augsburg, 1991.

Logan, Robert. *Beyond Church Growth.* Old Tappan, N.J.: Fleming H. Revell, 1989.

Luecke, David. *Evangelical Style and Lutheran Substance.* St. Louis: Concordia, 1988.

Luther, Martin. Article 349 of *Preachers and Preaching.* Quoted in *The Table Talk of Martin Luther*, ed. Thomas S. Kepler. New York: World, 1952.

McGinnis, Alan Loy. *The Power of Optimism.* San Francisco: HarperSanFrancisco, 1990.

———. *The Friendship Factor.* Minneapolis: Augsburg, 1979.

Maxwell, John. *Your Attitude: Key to Success.* San Bernardino, Calif.: Here's Life Publishers, 1984.

Mead, Loren. *The Once and Future Church.* Washington, D.C.: Alban Institute, 1991.

Murren, Doug. *The Baby Boomerang.* Ventura, Calif.: Regal Books, 1990.

Naisbitt, John. *Megatrends.* New York: Warner Books, 1982.

Naisbitt, John and Patricia Auberdene, *Megatrends 2000.* New York: Morrow, 1990.

Neuchterlein, Anne Marie. *Improving Your Multiple Staff Ministry.* Minneapolis: Augsburg, 1989.

Niebuhr, Gustave. "So It Isn't Rock of Ages, It Is Rock, and Many Love It." *Wall Street Journal*, Thursday, December 19, 1991.

Ogilvie, Lloyd John. *Praying with Power.* Ventura, Calif.: Regal Books, 1983.

Peters, Tom and Nancy Austin. *A Passion for Excellence: The Leadership Difference.* New York: Random House, 1985.

Peters, Tom and Robert Waterman Jr. *In Search of Excellence: The Leadership Difference.* New York: Random House, 1985.

———. *In Search of Excellence: Lessons from America's Best-Run Companies.* New York: Harper & Row, 1982.

Plagenz, George R. "Entertainment Issues Cause Split Among Lutherans." *Verde Independent*, Friday, October 12, 1990.

Postman, Neil. *Amusing Ourselves to Death.* New York: Viking, 1986.

Ramey, David. *Empowering Leadership.* Kansas City, Mo.: Sheed & Ward, 1991.

Rowlison, Bruce. *Creative Hospitality as a Means of Evangelism.* Campbell, Calif.: Green Leaf, 1981.

Rush, Myron. *Management: A Biblical Approach.* Wheaton, Ill.: Victor Books, 1983.

Sample, Tex. *White Soul: Country Music, the Church, and Working Americans*. Nashville: Abingdon, 1996.

Savage, John. *The Apathetic and Bored Church Member*. Pittsford, N.Y.: LEAD Consultants, 1976.

Schaller, Lyle E. *The Seven-Day-A-Week Church*. Nashville: Abingdon, 1992.

————. *Looking in the Mirror*. Nashville: Abingdon, 1984.

————. *The Multiple Staff and the Larger Church*. Nashville: Abingdon, 1992.

————. *Parish Planning*. Nashville: Abingdon, 1971.

————. *The Senior Minister*. Nashville: Abingdon, 1988.

Schineller, Peter. *A Handbook of Inculturation*. New York: Paulist, 1990.

Schuller, Robert. *Your Church Has a Fantastic Future!* Ventura, Calif.: Regal Books, 1986.

Senge, Peter. *The Fifth Discipline*. New York: Currency, 1991.

Shenk, Wilbert, ed. *The Challenge of Church Growth: A Symposium*. Scottdale, Pa.: Herald Press, 1973.

Smalley, Gary and John Trent. *The Language of Love*. Pomona, Calif.: Focus on the Family Publishing, 1988.

Stanford, Craig. *The Death of the Lutheran Reformation*. Fort Wayne, Ind.: Standford Publishing, 1988.

Steinke, Peter. "How Healthy Is Your Congregation?" *The Lutheran* (March 1995).

Swindoll, Charles. *Living Above the Level of Mediocrity*. Waco, Tex.: Word, 1987.

————. *Rise & Shine*. Portland: Multnomah, 1989.

————. *The Grace Awakening*. Dallas: Word, 1990.

Vaughan, John. *Church Growth Journal of the North American Society of Church Growth*. Bolivar, Mo.: 1990.

Wagner, C. Peter. *Leading Your Church to Growth*. Ventura, Calif.: Regal Books, 1984.

————. *Church Growth and the Whole Gospel*. London: MARC Europe, British Church Growth Association, 1981.

Wagner, C. Peter, ed., with Win Arn and Elmer Towns. *Church Growth State of the Art*. Wheaton, Ill.: Tyndale House, 1986.

Walker, Alan. *The Whole Gospel for the Whole World*. New York and Nashville: Abingdon, 1957. Quoted in George G. Hunter III, *How to Reach Secular People*.

Westfall, John. *Coloring Outside the Lines: Discipleship for the "Undisciplined."* San Francisco: HarperSanFrancisco, 1991.

Willard, Dallas. *The Spirit of the Disciplines*. New York: Harper & Row, 1988.